Courageous Dissent

The History Behind the Vietnam Warfighting Strategy and the Five Marine Generals Who Advocated Alternatives, 1965-1969

A.S. Kyle, G.M. Davis,
Robert Packard, John Cochenour

Copyright © 2023 A.S.Kyle

All rights reserved. No part of this publication may be reproduced or transmitted in any form or by any means, electronic or mechanical. including photocopy, recording, or any information storage and retrieval system without the written permission of the author except in the case of brief quotations embodied in critical articles and reviews. For rights and permissions contact the author: courageousdissent@gmail.org

Every effort has been made to ensure the accuracy of the information contained in this book at the time of its release. The book incorporates public domain material from websites or documents of the United States Marine Corps, the Department of the Navy, and National Archive. Unless otherwise noted in the caption, photographs are from the private collections of the authors or from the public domain images in the National Archives, USMC Military History Division or Department of Defense. Research, writing, editing, interior design, and cover were done by the authors.

ISBN: 979-8-9883610-0-8 (paperback)

Front Cover Photo: "Middle of Nowhere"—Marine UH-IE (Huey) helicopters touch down with their loads at Fire Support Base Cunningham. Artillerymen of the 12th Marines at Cunningham are supporting elements of the 9th Marines conducting operations in Operation Dewey Canyon. (Photo by LCpl M.C. Patterson) Sea Tiger, 28 February 1969, Vol. V, No. 9

Back Cover Photo: Lieutenant General Krulak briefing President Johnson in the White House Oval Office, August 1966. Photo SN A 3615-12A purchased from the National Archives.

Dedication

*To Deb, with love -
your encouragement and patience made this book possible*

Table of Contents

Preface	1
1st Lieutenant Davis (K Company, 3/9)	4
1st Lieutenant Cochenour (E Battery, 2/12)	5
1st Lieutenant Packard (Provisional Rifle Platoon, 2/3)	6
1st Lieutenant Kyle (HQ battery, 2/12)	6
Background, Pre-1965	7
Dissent	8
Historical Dissent	9
Contemporary Dissent	10
General Wallace Greene USMC	12
Lieutenant General Victor Krulak USMC	14
Major General Wood Kyle USMC	15
Major General Lowell English USMC	16
General Raymond "Ray" Davis USMC	18
Marine Dissent Events	19
Planning, 1965	23
House Armed Services Committee (HASC) Meeting	25
White House Conference	28
Presidential Press Conference	31
Strategies, 1966	35
Retrospective Evaluations of Early Strategies	35
Early Pacification Strategies	38
Early Warfighting Strategies	41
Presidential Briefings	43

The Barrier, 1967	47
The War in the North — NVA Infiltration	49
NVA Artillery - 1966, 1967	50
The Barrier Concept	51
The Barrier Conference	54
Barrier Construction	57
NVA Offensive	58
Proposal to Interdict the Ho Chi Minh Trail	60
Khe Sanh, 1968	63
Khe Sanh Background	64
The Siege at Khe Sanh, January 1968	68
The Siege at Khe Sanh, February 1968	80
Lang Vei	81
After Lang Vei	83
Outcomes	87
Dewey Canyon, 1969	91
"Before-Dark" Dictates	92
Operation Dewey Canyon Background	95
Phase I	98
Phase II	99
Phase III	105
Outcomes	111
Aftermath	115
Dissent Outcomes	117
Conclusion	120
Appendices	125
Appendix A	126
Appendix B	139
Appendix C	154
Appendix D	159

Appendix E	161
Author's Note	163
Glossary	166
List of Abbreviations	168
Bibliography	171
Acknowledgements	176

Preface

This book was shaped by many factors, but three elements are responsible for the energy necessary to write and publish it: the passage of time, reflection about the impact of the Vietnam War on our lives, and questions about why we failed. At the time of this writing, fifty years have passed since the Paris Peace Accords ended direct United States involvement in the Vietnam War and fifty-four years since the contributors to the book fought on the same battlefield together in Vietnam. After those fifty-plus years, battlefield experiences faded, and common memories were shelved. It wasn't until recently that social media, old- timer reunions, and retirements enabled this "band of brothers" to write this book.

This combination of perspective over time, opportunity to revive and relive memories, growing curiosity about the reasons for different decisions impacting assignments, movements, and engagements, all led to broader, deeper researching and reading. The insights we gained from our personal interactions have led us to share these stories with other Vietnam veterans and those interested in this piece of American history.

It is difficult to find a coherent, consistent, overriding mission statement that guided the United States efforts in Vietnam between 1955 and 1975. Some believe it was a noble struggle against Communist aggression—a war fought to prevent the domino effect of a cold war strategy. Others see it as a tragic intervention in a civil conflict which requires a generous view of South Vietnam as an independent nation. Many that protested the Vietnam War describe it as an American imperialist counter-revolution intended to suppress a struggle for national liberation. Inconsistencies in national policy and faulty assumptions contributed to our failure in aiding Vietnam. But what interested us was our warfighting strategies and how they may have contributed to our nation's long-term failure (or success). Perhaps most people agree that the Vietnam war was "unwinnable." We wonder, did bad war-plans and warfighting choices make the Vietnam war unwinnable?

What do we offer that will influence someone to read this account? We believe that many Americans are now open to new ways of understanding the Vietnam War. It was an extraordinarily critical event that influenced our nation's history. We believe scholarship on the war, both academic and popular history, is incomplete. Perhaps the best approach for explaining the Vietnam War is telling a story within the context of the warfighting strategies, the stories behind decisions leading to these strategies, and the dissents voiced by Marine generals tasked with the policy development or the employment of these strategies.

There have been many attempts to explain America's failure in Vietnam. David Halberstam blamed the President and his Staff, in *The Best and the Brightest*. Neil Sheehan blamed the nations' civilian and military leaders, in *A Bright Shining Lie*. H.R. McMaster blamed the Joint Chiefs of Staff, in *Dereliction of Duty*. Our approach is distinctive. We have avoided the more popular themes: counterinsurgency debates, unwinnable war theories, and the "blame game" of retrospective finger pointing. Instead, we focus on the warfighting strategies ordered by war managers in Washington, Saigon and the I Corps tactical zone. These strategies strongly influenced the conduct of the war, and Marine Generals dissented four of them, but failed to change strategic approaches. A fifth dissent by a Marine General resulted in commanders in I Corps employing a modified high-mobility strategy that achieved excellent results. This final dissent changed Marine warfighting strategies with the full support of U.S. Army superiors. If the war managers in Washington and Saigon had listened to generals on the ground earlier the conduct and outcome of the war might have had different results.

Also included is a brief history of a representative junior Marine officer. Mirza Munir Baig, or Harry, appeared in several parts of this story during our research phase. Although not a dissenter, he is an excellent example of the diversity of personalities in the Marine Corps. Baig was a brilliant and influential thinker with a recurring association with East Asia and Vietnam. In fact, one thread of this book is the degree to which Baig's life story tracks with key events of the Vietnam War.

Baig was personally involved with the Electronic Battlefield, including consulting with the technologies of sensors. This includes seismic intrusion devices (SIDS); the incredibly elaborate and expensive network (Muscle Shoals) used to collect, analyze, and report the sensor data; the role of the JASONS to develop the Electronic Battlefield; and Baig's use of the sensors at Khe Sanh. The book concludes with his intelligence work and the wind-down of the Vietnam war in Laos and Cambodia reflected in the Washington Special Acton Group (WSAG). These seminal events and developments of the Vietnam War can perhaps be grasped more clearly through the lens of Mirza Baig's life and career.

This book is written as a chronological narrative of selected warfare strategies and the characters involved. These strategies are identified as principal reasons for America's failure in Vietnam and are the focus of the book along with the challenges to their employment. The timeframe of these events is bookmarked by the arrival and departure of the first U.S. combat troops in Vietnam - the 9th Marine Regiment—an elite military organization, where all four writers of this book served as U.S Marine Lieutenants.

At the time, United States military forces in Vietnam were grouped under the combined headquarter of the Military Assistance Command, Vietnam (MACV). Immediately subordinate were five commands: U.S. Army-Vietnam, U.S, Naval Forces, Seventh Air Force, III Marine Amphibious Force (IIIMAF), and MACV Advisors. Geographically, South Vietnam was divided into four zones numbered I through IV running from the north to the south for the purpose of assigning administrative and command control of military operations. Much of the attention of this book focuses on actions in and around I Corps (pronounced 'Eye' Corps), the tactical zone of responsibility for the United States Marine Corps.

The Commanding General of the III Marine Amphibious Force controlled I Corps, which included some 98 maneuver battalions in early 1968. These units were from the U.S. Marine Corps, the U.S. Army, the Army of South Vietnam (ARVN) and the Republic of Korea. Most of the Marine battalions were operating from the Da Nang area northward to the Demilitarized Zone (DMZ). I Corps was nearest to North Vietnam and stretched some 350 miles from the DMZ south to include the five northern provinces of South Vietnam, as well as the major cities of Hue and Da Nang. In 1954, the DMZ was established by the Geneva Conference which ended the war between France and the Viet Minh. The zone ran from the South China Sea westward to Laos along the 17th parallel north and extended about a mile either side of the Ben Hai River.

Five appendices complete this book and are provided for the reader who wishes to dig deeper into the backgrounds and processes of the discussed decisions. Some are recently de-classified documents including memoranda for the record, reports, and exit interviews. These documents were selected to illustrate the details of the decision-making processes that contributed to America's failure in Vietnam, written by participants of those meetings. The general public may be less interested in these details; some scholars may be surprised by them.

For three days in February 1969, the four writers of this book crossed paths at Fire Support Base Cunningham, when the North Vietnamese Army attacked our base. Now, we are working together, from Massachusetts, Florida, California, and Colorado. We all served with the 9th Marines during 1968-1969 and experienced first-hand the consequences of both ill-planned war strategies and highly successful military operations. Our post-Vietnam careers were very different: U.S. Magistrate judge, Marine Lt. Colonel, university professor, and medical device entrepreneur. Our personal notes follow the Second Battalion, Twelfth Marines (2/12) *Command Chronology's* official summary of the attack on Cunningham, 17 February 1969.

> At 0430 hours on 17 February, the enemy launched an attack against FSB Cunningham which featured a coordinated mortar/sapper attack, RPG's, concussion grenades and satchel charges. The Battalion FDC was damaged (and the watch officer knocked unconscious) by several blasts which also scattered radios and FDC equipment; however, technical fire direction was automatically decentralized in accordance with standard instructions, and the battalion continued its mission without interruption. Centralized control was reestablished in about 30 minutes. One howitzer in Battery E was knocked out of action by a mortar round but was evacuated and replaced the following morning. 3,270 rounds were expended by 2/12 on self-defense missions, targets of opportunity, suspect assembly areas and likely escape routes between 0430 and 0730, including 88 I.C.M. and 59 beehive rounds direct fire. 37 enemy KIA were found within the position at first light. Casualties sustained were 3 KIA (including 2 DOW) and 17 WIA.

1st Lieutenant Davis (K Company, 3/9)

"It was February 17, 1969, and Operation Dewey Canyon was still hot. Earlier that morning we had been hit by an NVA ambush. I had been hit during the melee, and now had a hole in my hand which, left untreated, would quickly become infected. An hour later a resupply helicopter picked me up along with two wounded Marines from another platoon in our company. I have never been hit by lightning, but I think I felt something like it when the helicopter was suddenly jolted by a tremendous explosion. Somehow the pilot regained control and by some miracle we were still flying. The pilot headed north toward Fire Support Base Cunningham, about five miles away. The engines went silent. The helicopter dropped from several hundred feet, autorotating onto an LZ at Cunningham with a loud crunch. The helicopter was still there an hour later, when another helicopter took me to the field hospital. I had been hit once before, along the Da Krong River back in November '68. Now I had been shot through the hand, and the helicopter crash fractured a vertebra in my low back. The three injuries got me out of the jungle."

1st Lieutenant Cochenour (E Battery, 2/12)

"In the early morning of February 17, I was awake and had been talking with the XO's recorder before going out along the gun line. I was relaxed, my mind elsewhere when mortars began falling inside the position. We had been firing H&I's and the powder pits had not yet been emptied. A mortar round hit in gun one's pit and started a fire. The fire silhouetted running men and small arms fire began to erupt from our perimeter infantry and my own gun pits. I believe a satchel charge was slung into the gun one emplacement and the explosion destroyed that position—disabling the howitzer. We continued to defend the battery position with the other five howitzers using illumination, I.C.M. and beehive, plus our small arms fire until daylight. Our battery had four wounded Marines, three from gun one. We would medevac them and begin clean-up immediately, as two of the gun pits would need to be rebuilt— all would need repair. Bodies of enemy sappers and equipment were taken to a central collection point. I remember this battle as one characterized by surprise and reaction, by defensive plans and preparation, and by the courage and initiative of the individual Marine and non-commissioned officers. I believed it was a battle of some significance since I was involved, but it was only a small part of a very complex and successful operation. And ten days later the Dewey Canyon operation would have me and Echo Battery at FB Turnage atop Tiger Mountain."

Courageous Dissent

1st Lieutenant Packard (Provisional Rifle Platoon, 2/3)

"I was with a provisional rifle platoon ("every Marine is a rifle-man") that had been operating in and around Quang Tri for two or three weeks, as part of a provisional rifle company moving through town on trucks every day. We were "honored" to be diverted to FSB Cunningham for about 2 weeks more to help bolster the defenses there. The infantry battalion on FSB Cunningham was 2nd Battalion 3rd Marines. They gave us the side of the perimeter that was least susceptible to attack because it was so steep there. I don't remember seeing Cochenour there, so I'd guess that I was there a few days after the 17th. You (Kyle) were deeply immersed in trying to sort out a huge tangle of comm wire when I saw you being hounded by the XO. I do remember a USMC Huey making a bad forced landing and burning up one day. In fact, a couple of other Marines and I tried and failed to extricate the pilot. I don't know that it could have been 1stLt Davis' medevac."

1st Lieutenant Kyle (HQ battery, 2/12)

"My own memory is of waking up in my hole, where I slept by myself. At first, I thought the attack was just mortars, so I stayed put until I heard Vietnamese yelling and screaming. As I would later learn, many of the attacking NVA Sappers were heavily drugged, and that may account for the odd sounds. The Radio Chief— Corporal Frank Renner — arrived to the fire direction center (FDC) sooner than I did, and he helped restore radio communications. I recall being asked by Major Condon to find out about restoring wire communications to the 4.2" mortars, because of their importance in providing close fire support around the lines. Lance Corporal JC Dye and Pete Hyla had already gone out to do that, and I went to find out the results— which were successful. Cleaning up the next morning was more memorable, because of the number of sappers killed nearby the battalion Fire Direction Center. We lost one Marine in HQ battery, but fortunately none in the Communications platoon."

※ ※

Chapter I

Background
Pre-1965

> *There are roads which must not be followed, armies which must be not attacked, towns which must not be besieged, positions which must not be contested, commands of the sovereign which must not be obeyed.* —Sun Tzu

Events following World War II (WWII) had an enormous influence on the American War in Vietnam, its beginning, the middle, and the end. In the aftermath of WWII, there was a collapse of the alliance among the nations that combined to win that war. An open yet restricted rivalry developed between the United States and the Soviet Union, lasting until the dissolution of the USSR. This rivalry is usually identified as lasting from 1945 until 1991, although the seeds for what became known as the Cold War probably began during World War I. The 1968 Tet Offensive in Vietnam was at the mid-point of the Cold War.

The term, Cold War, was first used by George Orwell in an article he published in 1945. It commonly refers to the geopolitical tension during that period and because there was no large-scale fighting between the superpowers. Instead, they supported opposing sides in the major regional conflicts referred to as proxy wars. Examples of proxy wars during this period include the Soviet-Afghan War, the Korean War, and the Vietnam War. The growing fears that conventional war would result in a nuclear holocaust made the use of ideological proxy wars a safer way of exercising hostilities.

Officially, the conflict in Vietnam was between North Vietnam and South Vietnam. It lasted nearly 20 years from 1955 until 1975 and aggravated and amplified both the Laotian Civil War and Cambodian Civil War. As an ally of France and because of the rise of nationalism, the fear of communism, the policy of containment, and the domino theory, the United States provided substantial aid (billions of dollars during the French Indochina War).

Following the French military withdrawal from Indochina in 1954, a demarcation line along the 17th parallel which became the Demilitarized Zone was established by the Geneva Accords. The U. S. would assume financial and military support for South Vietnam. North Vietnam was controlled by the Viet Minh and supported by China, the Soviet Union, and other communist states. North Vietnam initiated a guerrilla war in the south by directing the National Liberation Front known as the Viet Cong (VC). The North Vietnamese Army (NVA) was the face of conventional warfare in direct conflicts with the South Vietnam army (ARVN), U.S. and allied forces.

A U.S State Department report in 1961 disclosed that landlocked, poverty-stricken Laos was the first foreign policy crisis President John Kennedy would have to face. He called for an end to hostilities in Laos and for negotiations with hopes of achieving an independent and neutralized Laos. These negotiations created time and opportunity for the NVA to conduct an offensive in southern Laos. North Vietnam had already invaded Laos in 1958 and built the Ho Chi Minh Trail to supply and reinforce the VC. With the new offensive in 1961, they captured "the crossroad village of Tchepone and the terrain necessary to extend the Ho Chi Minh Trail to the western side of the Annamite Mountains on the border between Laos and South Vietnam." This terrain, specifically Tchepone, proved to be an influencing element during the Vietnam War.

By 1963 North Vietnam had 40,000 NVA soldiers fighting in the south. Under John Kennedy's watch the U.S. increased from under 1,000 military advisors in 1959 to 23,000 by 1964. Decisions regarding the depth and breadth of our assistance to South Vietnam were shaped by the perceptions and actions of the Cold War participants and would continue to impact Cold War options and choices after 1975. While the Cold War would frame it, the Vietnam War would influence the later events of the Cold War. Laos, Cambodia, and Vietnam would all become communist states by 1975.

Dissent

The Cambridge Dictionary defines dissent as "a strong difference of opinion on a particular subject, especially about an official decision or suggestion or plan or a popular belief." In its verb form dissent means simply having a different opinion--to disagree, to challenge, to differ, to non-concur. The Cambridge

English Corpus suggests the following usage example: "Conflicts between local communities and multinational corporations, for example, may not be resolvable as series of compromises, but will require some clear and courageous decisions."

In a military context, we view dissent as holding or expressing an informed opinion that is at variance with an official view or with dominant ways of thinking. There are many kinds of dissent: disagreement with tactical/situational awareness on the battlefield, disagreements in civil-military interactions, disobeying "militarily absurd" orders, and loyal dissent—carefully thought-out and well-designed opinions to help the military accomplish their mission.

Many tough questions surround the idea of military dissent. Should dissent by military leaders be confined to the chain of command? Is dissent outside the chain of command appropriate? Should dissent against moral judgements be allowed? To call dissent "courageous," must there be consequences to the dissenter?" Do the Army and the Navy view dissent in the same way? Selected samples of past dissent by U.S. military leaders might help in answering these questions.

Historical Dissent

In 1783, General George Washington stopped soldiers of the Continental Army from carrying out a planned military action against the Congress. The Newburgh Conspiracy was resolved without violence. He persuaded the Congress that the soldiers' complaints were valid and consistent with the independence movement. Washington's dissent saved the nation.

Dissent is viewed differently by U.S. military services. The respective War colleges have a very strong influence, and so does the rule of law. In 1884, Admiral Stephen Luce founded the Naval War College. Since then, the Navy has been recognized as a service that tolerates dissent with established plans and policy and encourages its officers to represent their views openly and responsibly. The Navy's view is described in an article by Jimmy Brennan, "Bad Ideas Have No Rank: The Moral Imperative of Dissent in the Navy."

> In 1923, twenty-three sailors died in the waters off Honda Point, California, when Commodore Edward H. Watson errantly led his formation of 14 destroyers to disaster. It was the largest-ever peacetime loss of U.S. Navy ships. Despite heavy fog, inconsistent

navigational data, and a failure to take precautionary soundings, six captains followed his order to steam in close formation at high speed to exercise a wartime scenario. All those ships were lost. In the end, the general courts-martial held each of the six captains accountable for his decision to follow orders instead of trusting his own judgment.

Two captains disobeyed the order and managed to save their ships. The legal judgement encouraged dissent in the Naval Services.

The United States Army has been profoundly influenced by Professor Samuel Huntington of Harvard University. More than five decades ago, he noted in his classic book *The Soldier and the State: The Theory and Politics of Civil–Military Relations, 1957*, that loyalty and obedience are the cardinal military virtues. An act of public dissent is to be exceptionally rare. Huntington's teachings have remained embedded in the U.S. Army's professional ethos to this day.

Contemporary Dissent

A summary of dissent in the U.S. Army was given by Don M. Snider, in a 2008 paper on dissent and strategic leadership in the military. He wrote:

> The U.S. military has a long tradition of strong partnership between the civilian leadership of the Department of Defense and the uniformed services. Both have long benefited from a relationship in which the civilian leadership exercises control with the advantage of fully candid professional advice, and the military serves loyally with the understanding that its advice has been heard and valued. That tradition has been frayed, and civil military relations need to be repaired.

During the 1960s, Generals James Gavin (U.S. Army) and David Shoup (U.S. Marine Commandant from 1959 to 1963) were two military leaders who opposed the growing U.S. commitment to the Republic of Viet Nam. Historian Robert Buzzanco and others have described their dissent in detail. After retiring from their military careers and entering public life later in the decade, Shoup and Gavin became two of the most vocal critics of the U.S. war effort. Gavin appeared on television. Shoup spoke at a junior college convention. They wrote articles in national magazines and authored and edited widely reviewed books. Though they did not join Vietnam Veterans Against the War, these retired generals did take their anti-war views to the public. Shoup asserted that the Joint Chiefs of Staff had discussed sending troops to Viet Nam frequently. He said, "in every case... every senior officer that I knew... said we should never send ground combat forces into Southeast Asia."

In 2006, four retired generals—Gregory Newbold, Anthony Zinni and Paul Van Riper (U.S. Marines) and Paul Eaton (U.S. Army)—spoke publicly against Secretary of Defense Donald Rumsfeld's leadership of the war in Iraq. During the war in Iraq, when the retired generals assailed Rumsfeld's leadership, they said in public what their friends still in uniform were saying in private. The generals were worried about saving democracy in Iraq. They were joined by Generals John Riggs, Charles Swannack, and John Batiste (U.S. Army). "They only need the military advice when it satisfies their agenda," said Riggs. Swannack emphasized that Rumsfeld bore "culpability" for the abuses at Abu Ghraib. More than a decade later, they were joined by retired Admiral William McRaven (U.S. Navy), and Stanley McChrystal (U.S. Army) - former commander of U.S. and international forces in Afghanistan. He said in an ABC News interview that the President was both immoral and less than honest. Retired Admiral and former commander of the North Atlantic Treaty Organization (NATO) James Stavridis (U.S. Navy) wrote of a "sense that the President's moral structure was…unconventional to the military mind."

In 2017, James Mattis, Secretary of Defense and former General (U.S. Marines) gave the following guidance to the Department of Defense on handling matters of ethics, which permeate all decisions in the military.

> I expect every member of the Department to play the ethical midfield. I need you to be aggressive and show initiative without running the ethical sidelines, where even one misstep will have you out of bounds. I want our focus to be on the essence of ethical conduct: doing what is right at all times, regardless of the circumstances or whether anyone is watching. To ensure each of us is ready to do what is right, without hesitation, when ethical dilemmas arise, we must train and prepare ourselves and our subordinates. Our prior reflection and our choice to live by an ethical code will reinforce what we stand for, so we remain morally strong especially in the face of adversity. Through our example and through coaching of all hands, we will ensure ethical standards are maintained. Never forget, our willingness to take the Oath of Office

and to accept the associated responsibilities means that even citizens who have never met us trust us to do the right thing, never abusing our position nor looking the other way when we see something wrong.

James Mattis resigned in 2018 from his position as Secretary of Defense. He said: "I had no choice but to leave."

In 2019, John F. Kelly, retired Marine General, resigned from his post as the President's Chief of Staff. Kelly told the Los Angeles Times that he was proudest during his White House tenure of the things that he prevented the President from doing.

Lieutenant Commander Jimmy Drennan, president of the Center for International Maritime Security, added his thoughts on dissent in "Bad Ideas Have No Rank: The Moral Imperative of Dissent in the Navy," a July 2019 article in the U.S. Naval Institute:

> Passivity is not an option. Even when decisions do not involve an ethical dilemma, the moral imperative to voice dissent in the Navy still exists. Ours is a business of violence and death. To remain silent in the face of decisions you believe to be wrong equates to an immoral act, and you accept responsibility for the potential lethal consequences, however distant or remote they may be.

These officers believed their patriotic and responsible duty was to voice their dissent and express alternatives. The five Marine Generals whom we single out below dissented during the Vietnam War also belong in the above group. None of the five dissenters in Vietnam advanced their careers. All were voicing what they believed was right—regardless of whether anyone was watching.

General Wallace Greene USMC

Wallace Greene was born in 1907 in Waterbury, Vermont. He was a descendant of the family of Nathanael Greene, the Revolutionary War hero. Alexander Hamilton, referred to Nathanael Greene as "a universal and pervading genius." General Wallace Greene had much in common with his ancestor. Both were relatively small in stature but were huge military leaders and patriots. In 1925, Greene graduated from high school in Burlington, Vermont, then attended the University of Vermont for a year before entering the United States Naval Academy in Annapolis, Maryland. In 1930, Greene graduated and was com-

Backgroiund

missioned a second lieutenant in the United States Marine Corps.

Following training schools and sea duty, he sailed for Guam in October 1936 and was stationed there until 1937. He was then transferred to Shanghai, China and the 4th Marine Regiment as a "China Marine." Receiving a promotion to Captain, Greene was attached to the defense forces of the International Settlement during the Sino-Japanese hostilities of 1937 and 1938. This was the period of Japan's expansion into China, and the Marines helped provide security to the International Settlement. In 1941, he was ordered to London, England, as a Special Naval Observer. Greene attended the British Amphibious Warfare School, was promoted to major, and returned to the United States.

His service in WWII included the Marshall Islands invasion. He was awarded his first legion of Merit with combat "V", was promoted to lieutenant colonel, and joined the 2nd Marine Division, serving as the Operations Officer (G-3). He was awarded his second Legion of Merit during combat on Saipan and Tinian. Following the war, he was promoted to colonel and served as the G-3 of the Fleet Marine Force (Pacific). He also served in Quantico, the National War College, and the National Security Council.

In 1956, at the Marine Recruit Depot, Parris Island, South Carolina, six recruits drowned during an unauthorized night training march. The tragedy shook the Marine Corps to its foundations. As a brigadier general, Greene was put in charge of recruit training as the Commanding General, Recruit Training Command and later served as Commanding General of the base. He ended long-standing practices such as mass punishments and physical abuse of recruits. In 1958, Greene reported to Headquarters Marine Corps as Assistant Chief of Staff, G-3. While serving in this capacity, he was promoted to major general. He served as Deputy Chief of Staff (plans), then Chief of Staff, with the rank of lieutenant general.

In 1963, President John F. Kennedy named Greene to become the 23rd Commandant of the Marine Corps and promoted to four-star rank. During his first year as Commandant, General Greene had a front row seat watching a small group of civilians—including Secretary of Defense McNamara, and McGeorge Bundy, Special Assistant to the President for National Security Affair—recommending decisions which primarily involved the military. Greene believed that this group was seeking easy and simple solutions to an increasingly complex problem that centered around the viability and sovereignty of the Vietnamese people.

During 1964, Greene made both public and private proposals for the creation of what he variously called a "National Staff" or a "National General Staff." The plan called for the creation of a large, permanently constituted staff of military and civilian personnel tasked with the sole purpose of studying potential national security problems and devising appropriate policy solutions to those challenges. Though a civilian-operated organization, the National Staff would function in a similar manner to a military staff and manage a National Command Center. General Greene was a very experienced officer, that spoke his mind and worked through the chain of command.

Lieutenant General Victor Krulak USMC

Victor Krulak was born in Denver, Colorado in 1913 to Jewish parents, Bessie (Zall) and Morris Krulak. In 1934, Krulak graduated from the Naval Academy and was commissioned a Second Lieutenant in the Marine Corps.

One of Krulak's first assignments was coxswain in Navy's unsuccessful eight-man boat at the Olympic trials in Princeton, New Jersey. Krulak also served with the 4th Marines in China (1937–39) and took photographs with a telephoto lens of a ramp-bowed landing boat that the Japanese had been using. Recognizing the potential use of such a craft by the United States' armed forces, Krulak sent details and photographs back to Washington, but discovered years later that they had been filed away as having come from "some nut out in China." Undeterred, Krulak built a model of the Japanese boat design and discussed the retractable ramp approach with boat builder Andrew Higgins who incorporated elements of Krulak's input into the Landing Craft, Vehicle, Personnel (LCVP) or "Higgins boat," which played critical roles in the Normandy landings and amphibious assaults in the Pacific. The Higgins boat was involved in every World War II amphibious assault.

In WWII, Krulak served as battalion commander of the 2nd Parachute Battalion, 1st Marine Amphibious Corps. As a Lieutenant Colonel he earned the Navy Cross and the Purple Heart on Choiseul Island. The Navy PT boat, PT-59, captained by John F. Kennedy, helped evacuate Krulak's force from Choiseul at the end of the operation. In response, Krulak promised

Kennedy a bottle of whiskey which he delivered almost 20 years later when Kennedy was serving as President of the United States. After the war, Krulak served as assistant director of the Senior School at Marine Corps Base Quantico and as commander of the 5th Marines at Camp Pendleton.

In Korea, Krulak served as Chief of Staff, 1st Marine Division. In Washington, he served as Secretary of the General Staff, then rejoined Fleet Marine Force (Pacific) as Chief of Staff. In 1956, he was promoted to Brigadier General and was Assistant Commanding General, 3rd Marine Division in Okinawa and Director, Marine Corps Educational Center in Quantico, Virginia.

In Washington, D.C., Krulak served as special assistant for counter insurgency activities, on the Joint Chiefs of Staff. Following the assassination of President Kennedy, President Lyndon B. Johnson chose Krulak to head an interdepartmental group to select targets that the United States could hit in North Vietnam with the least amount of risk to its people. In 1964, Krulak was designated Commanding General, Fleet Marine Force, Pacific, and promoted to Lieutenant General. For the next four years, Krulak would make 54 trips to Vietnam.

Robert Komer had a good description of Krulak in his book *Brute*, "He adhered to the French military expression 'De l'audace, encore de l'audace, et toujours de l'audace'." This translates to audacity, more audacity, and audacity forever.

Major General Wood Kyle USMC

Wood Kyle was born in Pecos, Texas in 1915. He graduated from Texas A&M and was commissioned as a Second Lieutenant in the United States Marine Corps in 1936. Following Officer Training at the Basic School, he embarked for China. Like Greene and Krulak, Kyle was a China Marine, serving as a platoon leader stationed on the Suzhou Creek in Shanghai. After returning to the United States, he served aboard the aircraft carrier USS Lexington.

In WWII, he served as a battalion executive officer for 1st Battalion Second Marines on Guadalcanal and assumed command when the battalion commander was seriously wounded. For his actions at Guadalcanal, Kyle received a Silver Star and Purple Heart. He received a second Silver Star and promotion to lieutenant colonel at the battle of Tarawa in 1943. He led his battalion in the battles of Saipan and Tinian. After his return to the United States, he attended the Army Command and General Staff College and served as an instructor on the faculty.

Following the General Staff College, his assignments included service at the Pacific Headquarters at Pearl Harbor, attendance at the Army War College at Carlisle, Pennsylvania, and service at the Marine Development Center in Quantico. In 1958, he was appointed Chief of Joint Plans at the U.S. Headquarters in Paris, France. He was promoted to brigadier general in 1961 and ordered back to the United States where he commanded Force Troops at Camp Lejeune, North Carolina. He then did a three-year tour in Washington DC as Deputy Chief of Staff for Research and Development.

Promoted to Major General, he was ordered to South Vietnam in 1966 as Commanding General, 3rd Marine Division. During October, Kyle would have multiple tasks to contend with. This included an order to shift Marine units, including his 3rd Marine Division, to prevent a possible North Vietnamese push across the Demilitarized Zone (DMZ) in the northernmost part of South Vietnam. For the first time, an army infantry unit was added to the Marine Sector in the Vietnam War. The 3rd Marine Division moved their headquarters from Da Nang to Phu Bai. At the same time, and in the midst of extraordinarily heavy fighting, the Barrier Study Conference was held at the Marine Base in Da Nang. The conference was attended by dozens of "VIPs" from Saigon and the United States.

Secretary of Defense McNamara and General Westmoreland attended the conference, did an observation flight in a helicopter along the DMZ to Khe Sanh, and agreed on a 30km long barrier now named the 'strong point system' in the eastern portion of the DMZ area. The barrier conference was an opportunity for the uniformed military to dissent the barrier concept and advocate the alternative of an "active defense" strategy.

In his 226-page Oral History, General Kyle described his experience fighting in China, and in the Pacific Islands where he fought as an infantry battalion commander on Guadalcanal, Tarawa, and Saipan. Over that highly eventful period, he dissented relatively little. For his year in Vietnam, he strongly criticized the poor-quality intelligence provided to the Marines from MACV headquarters in Saigon.

Background

Major General Lowell English USMC

Lowell English was born in Fairbury, Nebraska in 1915. In 1938, he graduated from the University of Nebraska, where he played guard on the Cornhusker's championship football team. He turned down an offer to play professional football with the Chicago Bears and completed Marine officer training in 1939.

English's service in WWII began as a company commander. He fought in Guam and was decorated with the Bronze Star Medal with Combat "V". He was quickly promoted and served as a Lieutenant Colonel at Iwo Jima as Commanding Officer of 2nd Battalion, 21st Marines.

English would later recall a situation on Iwo Jima. His regiment had landed under heavy enemy fire. Progress was slow and costly, and his Battalion suffered heavy casualties. English was himself wounded when a Japanese bullet went through his knee. As his battalion was being rotated to the rear, English received orders to turn his men around and plug a gap in the front lines. He was dismayed by the order and described the situation.

> I couldn't move that disorganized battalion a mile back north in 30 minutes. We had taken very heavy casualties and were pretty well disorganized. I had less than 300 men left out of the 1200 I came ashore with. The Commanding General of 3rd Marine Division did not want excuses, and he told English's Regimental Commander. "You tell that damned English he'd better be there." English then fired back, "You tell that son of a bitch I will be there, and I was, but my men were still half a mile behind me, and I got a blast through the knee."

For his service on Iwo Jima, English was decorated with the Legion of Merit with Combat "V" and received the Purple Heart for his wounds. Needless to say, not many lieutenant colonels called their Division Commander a "son of a bitch."

Following WWII, English served for three years as military psychology and leadership instructor at the Naval Academy in Annapolis, followed by three years in the same position at the Military Academy in West Point, New York, and one year as instructor and student at the Armed Forces Staff College at Norfolk, Virginia.

In 1953, English served in Korea as Executive Officer of the 1st Marine Regiment, as Commanding Officer of the 3rd Battalion, 1st Marines, and as Marine Liaison Officer of U.S. Eighth Army under Lieutenant General Maxwell Taylor. After

Korea, English was promoted to colonel and served as Chief of Staff, Marine Corps Recruit Depot, San Diego, Commanding Officer of The Basic School in Quantico, VA, and was an instructor at the Army War College at Carlisle Barracks, Pennsylvania. Transferred to Washington D.C., English served under Paul Nitze in the Office of Assistant Secretary of Defense for International Security Affairs and earned a master's degree in International Relations at George Washington University. He was promoted to brigadier general in August 1963, moved to London, England and served as Chief of Staff, U.S. Naval Forces, Eastern Atlantic and Mediterranean. He returned to the United States in January 1964 and was Deputy Chief of Plans of United States Strike Command in Florida.

English was ordered to South Vietnam in 1965. In 1966, Marine reconnaissance reported the presence of the NVA 324th Division in the vicinity of the Demilitarized Zone. English received orders from then 3rd Division Commander General Wood Kyle to activate Task Force Delta. This task force included four infantry battalions, one artillery battalion and various supporting forces. English used Delta in combined attacks of ground forces, artillery, airstrikes, and helicopter assaults to kill approximately 700 NVA soldiers. The Marines suffered 126 killed and many wounded. Operation Hastings was followed by Operation Prairie in August 1966, and English continued to lead Task Force Delta. However during 1966, General English was ordered to deploy one of his Marine battalions to defend Khe Sanh, a problematic order for English. General Lowell English was known throughout his career as an intelligent and outspoken officer.

General Raymond "Ray" Davis USMC

Ray Davis was born in 1915, in Fitzgerald, Georgia. He attended the Georgia Institute of Technology, graduating in 1938 with a Bachelor of Science degree in Chemical Engineering, and accepted an appointment as a Marine Corps Second Lieutenant in 1938. Davis completed Marine officer training at The Basic School in 1939, after which he was assigned to one year of sea duty and weapons instruction. Following his promotion to captain he served as a battery commander with an anti-aircraft machine gun battery.

During WW II, Davis served in Guadalcanal and Eastern New Guinea. In 1944 on Cape Gloucester, he was named as the

Commanding Officer of the 1st Battalion, 1st Marine Regiment. During the first hour of the landing at Peleliu, he was wounded. He refused evacuation and on one occasion, due to heavy Marine casualties and point-blank Japanese cannon fire, the Japanese broke through the lines, and he personally rallied and led his men in fighting to re-establish defensive positions. Davis' heroism at Peleliu earned him the Navy Cross and the Purple Heart Medal. In October 1944, he and his battalion returned to Pavuvu Island, and he was promoted to lieutenant colonel.

After his service in the Pacific Campaign, he was named Chief of the Infantry Section, Quantico in 1945, and served in that post for two years before returning to Guam in the Pacific area. In 1949, he was named Inspector-Instructor of the 9th Marine Corps Reserve Infantry Battalion in Chicago, Illinois until 1950 when he embarked for South Korea.

During the Korean War, Davis commanded the 1st Battalion 7th Marines. In the battle to break out of the Chosin Reservoir, surrounded by Chinese soldiers, he marched his battalion at night over mountains in a driving snowstorm, and saved Fox Company, 2nd Battalion 7th Marines from annihilation. For this action he was awarded the Medal of Honor. It was presented to Davis by President Harry S. Truman in a White House ceremony in 1952. Davis was also awarded two Silver Star Medals for gallantry in action, and the Bronze Star Medal with Combat "V" for his part in rebuilding the 7th Regiment in South Korea after the Chosin Reservoir campaign.

Following the Korean War, Davis had assignments at Marine Headquarters, the Senior Course in Quantico, the National War College in Washington, D.C., and Chief of the Analysis Branch for the U.S. Commander, Europe in Paris, France. Returning to Asia, Davis served as Commanding General, SEATO in the Philippines during 1964. Davis was promoted to major general in 1966.

Transferred to Vietnam, Davis became Commanding General of the Third Marine Division in 1968. By this time, Secretary McNamara and General Westmoreland had left Vietnam. However, there remained a standing order for the Marines to man and defend the bases along the DMZ. General Ray Davis was widely known and admired, inside and outside the Marine Corps. He was one of most highly decorated combat veterans in American military history. General Davis was a courageous innovator and a "doer."

Marine Dissent Events

War Planning Strategy 1965 – General Wallace Greene

President Johnson, Secretary of Defense McNamara, and the Chairman of the Joint Chiefs of staff avoided a realistic and critical estimate of force levels, the likely duration, and potential casualties of the Vietnam War. General Greene, Commandant of the Marine Corps, disagreed with this position and stated his opinion directly to both the President and the other members of the Joint Chiefs in 1965. General Greene's estimate of the costs of the Vietnam War was extraordinarily accurate. His dissent and recommendations were ignored.

Attrition Strategy 1966 – Lieutenant General Victor Krulak

The President, Secretary of Defense and Chairman of the Joint Chiefs of staff all agreed to the military strategy of attrition, also known as search and destroy, and de-emphasized the need for pacification. Lt. General Krulak disagreed and told the Commanding General of Military Assistance Command Vietnam, the Secretary of Defense, and the President in August 1966 of his objections. Krulak's objection of the attrition approach, and advocacy for a combined military/warfighting and civilian/pacification strategy was ignored. At the beginning of the war, Krulak advocated the "Spreading Inkblot Theory." Later in the war, Krulak strongly opposed the establishment of the Khe Sanh Combat Base. In 1966, Krulak met with President Johnson in the Oval Office and dissented the attrition strategy. Krulak's recommendations and dissent was ignored.

Barrier Strategy 1967—Major General Wood Kyle

The anti-infiltration barrier proposal was the idea of Secretary of Defense McNamara and was opposed by virtually all military leaders in the chain of command—including Marines and the Navy Commander in the Pacific. The most specific and detailed objection to the barrier was delivered at the Barrier Study Conference in October 1966—a written "non-concur" response by Major General Kyle, Commanding General of the 3rd Marine Division. His non-concur report stated a mobile force of one Division would be a much more effective approach, saving lives and money. The Marines' dissent, including General Kyle, was ignored.

Strong Point Strategy 1968—Major General Lowell English

Defending Khe Sanh—like the barrier proposal—was opposed by Marine military leaders beginning with a 1966 War Game exercise that recommended against the idea. Like their opposition to the barrier, the Marines' dissent was nearly unanimous. The most detailed and comprehensive objection to the decision to defend Khe Sanh was voiced by Marine Major General English to the Fleet Marine Force Pacific staff in January 1967, one year before the siege of Khe Sanh began. It was estimated that one thousand Americans lost their lives defending Khe Sanh, months before the site was abandoned to the North Vietnamese. The Marines' dissent, including General English, was ignored.

High-Mobility Strategy 1969—General Ray Davis

General Davis' significant decision to implement the high-mobility strategy violated the order to man strong points across the DMZ. Davis re-oriented the Third Marine Division using the same high-mobility concepts demonstrated by the U.S. Army in Operation Pegasus during the withdrawal from the Khe Sanh position. The successes resulting from this strategic shift, as demonstrated by Operation Dewey Canyon, avoided corps-sized search and destroy operations aimed at NVA forces. Instead, Dewey Canyon would be a regimental-sized raid aimed at enemy logistics along the Laotian border. Davis' dissent via the chain of command, with support by his U.S. Army bosses, challenged the then existing warfighting strategy. His strategic recommendation was implemented, not ignored.

※ ※

Courageous Dissent

Chapter 2

Planning
1965

No one starts a war--or rather, no one in his sense ought to do so--without first being clear in his mind what he intends to achieve by the war and how he intends to conduct it." — Carl Von Clausewitz

After being nominated by President John F. Kennedy in September 1963, General Wallace Greene was promoted to four stars when he assumed the post of the 23rd Commandant of the Marine Corps on 1 January 1964. In his previous job, General Greene had served as Chief of Staff to General David Shoup, then Commandant of the Marine Corps (CMC), and had stood in for him in meetings with the Joint Chief of Staffs during the Kennedy administration. General Greene's other assignments had included the National Security Council (NSC) in 1953 during the Eisenhower era and at Headquarters Marine Corps (HQMC) in 1958. Those tours and 34 years of service had given the 57-year-old Annapolis graduate a close and personal view of the workings of the Pentagon, Congress, and the White House. During that time, he had watched the steady diminution of morale of the heads of the military: Chief of Naval Operations, Commandant of the Marine Corps and Chiefs of Staff of the Army and Air Force. Loss of autonomy among the senior military was matched by strained personal relationships between the military chiefs and with civilian officials in the executive branch, especially Defense Secretary Robert McNamara. General Greene glumly observed that the Joint Chiefs of Staff (JCS) influence had reached a new low.

The chaotic, disorganized, and overly politicized approach to national security policy was anathema to General Greene, who had built a career on diligent and thorough staff work. Throughout his career, Greene gained a reputation as a brilliant staff officer, a long-range planner and troubleshooter. General

Greene made detailed notes and reports which he relied upon for history, meetings, and planning. These notes and reports survive in the National Archives and were essential research in writing this book. Selected memoranda of General Greene from July 1965 are included in Appendix A.

By August of 1964, United States' support to South Vietnam included about 15,000 military advisors, and North Vietnam was receiving substantial aid from both China and the Soviet Union. Following a report of U. S. Navy ships being fired upon in the Gulf of Tonkin, President Lyndon Johnson ordered retaliatory air strikes against North Vietnam and asked Congress to pass a resolution supporting his actions. The Tonkin Gulf Resolution was passed stating, "Congress approves and supports the determination of the President, as Commander in Chief, to take all necessary measures to repel any armed attack against the forces of the United States and to prevent further aggression." All but two senators voted for the Tonkin resolution, and the House of Representatives vote was unanimous, based on the presumption that the resolution would help avoid a major war in Southeast Asia. Years later, it was determined that the destroyers had been on electronic intelligence missions that carried them into waters claimed by North Vietnam. Amid confusion and public pressure, Congress would later repeal the Tonkin Gulf Resolution.

In early 1965 General Greene regarded the situation in South Vietnam to be worse than at "any time in the past since we entered the country." Before determining any solution to problems in South Vietnam, he would recommend examining what was at stake for the United States and then whether we were willing to pay the price in acting on a solution. He described three categories of those stakes: National Security, pledges to South Vietnam, and the global prestige of the United States.

He determined the most important of these stakes was that of National Security and withdrawing from South Vietnam at that point would "simply be delaying a final accounting with the Communist side." He encouraged a strong effort to explain the nature of what was at stake to the American people, and he felt most people would elect to stay the course and pay the price. Importantly, General Greene also believed if the decision was to stay with South Vietnam and our commitments, then it was nec-

Planning

General Wallace Greene, Commandant USMC, 1963-1967

essary, and responsible, to choose a strategy that would lead to winning.

House Armed Services Committee (HASC) Meeting

A meeting was set for the early morning of 15 July 1965 for members of the JCS with the HASC Policy Subcommittee. It was held in the Office of Chairman Rivers in Room 2118 in the Rayburn House Office Building. HASC Chairman L. Mendel Rivers would preside over the meeting, while two important players were absent. JCS Chairman General Earl Wheeler and Secretary of War Robert McNamara were in Saigon, South Vietnam visiting General Westmoreland, Commanding General of the Military Assistance Command Vietnam (MACV). The meeting marked the first-time members of Congress would hear directly from the service Chiefs.

Attending the meeting were four members of the JCS: Admiral McDonald of the Navy, General Johnson of the Army, General McConnell of the Air Force, and General Greene of the Marines. Also in attendance were five members of the Committee: Chairman Rivers of SC, and the following members of Congress; Bates of MA, Hebert of LA, Philbin of MA, and Price of IL. HASC Chief Counsel John Blandford also attended. The Congressmen attending the meeting were primarily interested in the service chiefs' views of force levels—the estimated number of troops that would be required in the Vietnam War.

Discussions over civic action and combined operations were brief as General Greene described the Combined Action Program (CAP) in I Corps and the Marine's Popular Force Platoons (PFP). These operations were beneficial in providing important intelligence among other things. The PFP had been very successful as the Marines integrated a Vietnamese platoon or company with similar-sized Marine units under a single commander. Chairman Rivers was of the opinion the only way our operations could succeed in South Vietnam was through integrating the South Vietnamese into U.S. Forces.

The remaining four subjects (mobilization, troop levels, actions in North Vietnam, and immediate recommendations) would receive more detailed focus. Rivers asked each of the service chiefs to answer the question of each services personnel requirements for an escalating situation and whether or not mobilization would be necessary. General Greene:

> I stated that the Marine Corps had an immediate requirement for approximately 14,000 officers and enlisted men and that if the situation continued to escalate and more Marine Corps forces were required, that the Marine Corps would then need approximately 150,000 more officers and enlisted. I pointed out to the Chairman that at the present time we had some 28,000 Marines committed to South Vietnam with portions of the 1st Marine Division committed, in addition to the 3d Marine Division/1st Wing Team; that we have been able to establish (1) three secure areas-these secure areas in I CORPS, that in my opinion was desirable to join these secure areas into an amphibious coastal enclave as soon as possible, and that if it were to be done, it would require at least 150,000 more officers and men for the Marine Corps.

Questions for the other service chiefs and discussion followed. Admiral McDonald felt that 40,000 additional personnel would serve, but the Army and Navy were vaguer and less certain. After continued discussion and estimates, General Greene summed up that a total of at least 500,000 U.S. troops would be required. No one reacted.

The meeting went on to discuss any actions that should be directed towards North Vietnam. Concerns were expressed about Haiphong, Haiphong Harbor and a bridge that crosses the river near Haiphong. The Surface-to-Air Missile (SAM) sites and IL-28 Beagle bombers near Hanoi were also noted as important targets. These were important supply and strategic targets, and Chairman Rivers and Mr. Blandford had questions about why no recommendations for interdicting these targets had been made. The Navy and Air Force Chiefs provided explanations that these targets had been identified but no action taken because of political considerations and concerns about alienating allies that used Haiphong Harbor. General Greene notes that he believed these excuses were not truthful since at least one of the targets had been put forward several times for bombing but had been rejected by the Secretary of the Defense or the White House.

At the close of the meeting, recommendations were made to intensify operations in both North and South Vietnam. Members of the HASC also made a point of telling the Joint Chiefs that they were highly respected, and the Committee wanted to ensure the necessary forces were provided. However, it was necessary for the JCS to provide "their opinions without fear or favor," and to remember that they had a duty to Congress as well as the Executive Branch. It was quickly pointed out by General Johnson that they were bound by the National Security Act of 1957, which tied the JCS solely to the Executive Branch. General Greene provided further explanation:

> ...the Chiefs were required to provide advice to the President and the Secretary of Defense. If this advice was not accepted by the President and the Secretary of Defense, when the Joint Chiefs and the Commandant were called over — as they were this morning to consult with the Committee — the Chiefs found themselves in a very difficult position between the Committee and the Administration.

The meeting ended at 0820, and General Greene went home to eat some breakfast before going to the office. After arriving at his HQMC office at 1030, Greene made a call to John Blandford. Blandford was Counsel to Mendel Rivers, Chairman of the House Armed Services Committee (HASC). Blandford and Greene had both attended the HASC Policy Subcommittee meeting. Greene was concerned about the meeting and called Blandford to clarify information on projected costs and casualties of the Vietnam War which had been discussed earlier that day. Blandford and Greene had been friends for more than twenty years. They had served with the Marines in the Pacific during WW II. While working full time on the HASC staff, Blandford would achieve the rank of major general in the Marine Corps Reserve. Blandford was the current Chief Counsel but would eventually serve as HASC Chief of Staff.

Together they reviewed the items that represented the situation in Vietnam. Greene emphasized and reiterated that unless a political solution to the situation in South Vietnam was reached immediately, the following things would result: (1) a major war between the U.S. and the communist side, (2) a campaign of several years—at least five, (3) a large number of casualties for the United States, (4) a general mobilization (5) a minimum of 500,000 U.S. troops, and 6) an immediate intensification of operations in both North and South Vietnam. Blandford was a close confidant of HASC Chairman Rivers, and undoubtedly informed Rivers of the details of that call.

There was no question in General Greene's mind about the threat of a war in Vietnam, and he wanted to make sure that the leaders of Congress also understood that threat. Any suggestion that the Joint Chiefs of Staff was not honest with leaders of Congress was false. General Greene was clear, and remarkably accurate, in his estimates for the Vietnam War.

White House Conference

A week after the HASC meeting a conference on Southeast Asia was held at the White House. Again, the JCS members were present as were the service Secretaries and the Secretary of Defense. Members of the White House Staff were also present, but President Lyndon Johnson was running late. Secretary of Defense McNamara opened the meeting with a discussion regarding what he needed to be considered. Essentially, this was to answer two questions: what alternatives are possible, and which will "win" or what will be accomplished?

Secretary of the Navy Nitze spoke first and asked questions about how troops would be employed. He stated his study of the situation indicated more troops will be required than what was currently allocated under MACV's 34 Battalion Plan which was the current guiding document. This was an escalation building to 34 battalions including units from the United States, South Vietnam, South Korea, and Australia. This plan set expected budgetary requests and found acceptable a call-up of reserves and extension of tours of duty if necessary. General Greene agreed with this assessment and reiterated his assessment of a need for 100,000 U.S. troops to meet operational commitments in I-Corps. As the discussion continued, Greene wrote in his notes, "The great uncertainty— how do you pacify the country? Previous plans haven't worked—haven't met the goal."

Ten minutes into discussions the meeting was interrupted by President Johnson who brought in the British Ambassador for introductions, and then both left. Chairman of the Joint Chiefs General Wheeler reported that General Westmoreland, MACV, was asking to change the plan to 44 battalions in order to establish secure base areas and a reaction force. President Johnson returned to the meeting and was told the Joint Chiefs were still reviewing requirements for call-ups and budgets. Secretary McNamara moved to outline the proposed courses of actions and indicated his personal choice. "Expand promptly and substantially the U.S. military pressure against the Viet Cong in the South."

The President then went around the table asking each individual to share their views. While others were speaking General Greene gathered his thoughts. He believed it was essential to speak directly and fully to the President and deliver clearly what the Marine Corps position was. When he his turn came, Greene laid out a very detailed and complete statement of that position and his thinking.

He began with a clarifying statement about the situation in South Vietnam. It was not hopeless, but it was bad. However, solutions could be found if "we are willing to pay the price." He then outlined his views and recommendations within three categories of concerns. National security was the most important concern and withdrawal was only delaying a final accounting. Secondly, if we didn't honor our pledge with South Vietnam then we would face the Communist threat someplace else at a higher price. Not everyone wants to honor the pledge to South Vietnam since keeping the pledge will be costly. Lastly U.S. prestige would suffer if we were to abandon our commitment.

Greene believed the majority of Americans would back a decision to stay and pay the price and advised the President to make a truthful explanation of what was at stake regarding their national security. If they were aware and educated, he would have their support. Assuming his decision would be to stay the course in South Vietnam, it was important to turn to a winning strategy. He divided his strategic recommendations into two parts: South Vietnam and North Vietnam.

In South Vietnam, the Marines were already 28,000 strong in three coastal areas of I Corps. Greene advocated a strategy

The division of South Vietnam into four Corps Tactical Zones or Military Regions, plus a Special Capital Zone, was for administrative and tactical operations command purposes. I (eye) Corps was the northernmost region composed of 5 provinces.

that would introduce additional Marines in order to expand the three coastal areas into a single enclave.

> I believe that a total of 100,000 Marines, two Divisions and one Wing, will be necessary to establish this enclave. If this action is taken the lines of communication (i.e. the north-south railroad and the main north-south highway) can be secured and what is more important is that approximately 30% of all of the people in South Vietnam can be made secure within this enclave. I feel that this enclave technique can likewise be applied to the other three Corps areas. I realize that because of the more unfavorable terrain conditions in the other Corps areas that it will take more men and time to establish adequate enclaves. However, I firmly believe that this method can be applied successfully to all four Corps areas.

General Greene also believed the Combined Action Program (CAP) his Marines were conducting needed to continue to operate alongside any military action. A liberated enclave area

Planning

provided the necessary security for numerous aid programs such as medical, infrastructure, and nutrition. Military security and civil aid were intertwined. Greene reported that this approach was convincing villagers that Marines were there to help and blunting Viet Cong efforts. He then presented his recommendations regarding actions in North Vietnam.

> Now as to the strategy in the North, I agree with the Chief of Staff of the Air Force that we have not been successful there because we have not been hitting the right targets. As a specific example: I believe that the supplies which are large and located in the Port of Haiphong area should be destroyed. There are millions of gallons of fuel located in these storage areas and that fuel is being used in motor vehicles and for other purposes to carry the war against us in South Vietnam. Although I am an amateur at politics, I fail to understand why, when we know that at least one hard core regular North Vietnamese Division is operating against our forces in South Vietnam, that we hesitate for political reasons to bomb the POL dumps near Hanoi and Haiphong. I believe that this type of target can be destroyed with a minimum loss of civilian lives. I also feel that the MIGS and IL-28's located on the in North Vietnam should be destroyed. Furthermore, when the SAM sites become operational, they should also be attacked. I believe that the bridges northwest of Hanoi should be bombed and, finally the industrial targets, i.e., the factories and other industrial installations which have taken the North Vietnamese ten years to develop, should be destroyed after the targets which I have just described have been hit.

General Greene went on to express his recommendations to blockade the harbor in Haiphong and the Port of Sihanoukville, Cambodia. His research indicated that significant amounts of war materials were trafficked through Cambodia. He closed his statement with his estimate of what the price would be to win a victory in South Vietnam if the proper strategic decisions were made. "I feel that it will take a minimum of 5 years and will require at least 500,000 U.S. troops. If you will tell the people what our stakes in South Vietnam are, the majority of them will back you in the action which I have just described."

Presidential Press Conference

The week following his Southeast Asia meeting with the JCS, President Johnson held a mid-day press conference on 28 July at the White House. Johnson timed the speech for the noon hour in Washington, when there would be relatively few television viewers. He began with a statement in which he explained that U.S. involvement in the conflict in Vietnam would be expanded. The Joint Chiefs of Staff would begin implementation of the President's decision by approving the deployment of the Air Mobile Division and the 9th Marine Amphibious Brigade to South Vietnam. Strength after these deployments would be 125,000 and more would be sent if required. He also said that he'd decided not to call up the reserves. He spoke of the effect that the Vietnam War might have on the U.S. economy, relations with foreign countries, the possibility of hostilities escalating into a larger war, and his commitment to negotiate with the Viet Cong at "any time, any place." But the press conference was a lost opportunity for the President to inform the American people about the rationale for escalating the Vietnam war.

What General Greene had recommended, and the President failed to do was:
- Explain the national security risk. If the US were to withdraw from South Vietnam, we would have to confront the communist threat in some other place in Southeast Asia or even India, the Middle East or Africa. The longer we delay, the higher the cost.
- Tell the American people that our pledge to South Vietnam should be honored; the prestige of the U.S. before the rest of the world depended on it.
- Describe the strategy needed to win in South Vietnam: a military component and a civil affairs component.

The Russians and the Communist Chinese had been targeting less-developed nations throughout the world, adopting the aggressive doctrine of "wars of national liberation" as a vehicle for communist encirclement of the U.S. and Western Europe. Southeast Asia was a target in that struggle. In contrast, the U.S. containment policy rejected that notion worldwide, and supported the provisions of the 1962 Geneva agreements—specifically in Laos. The Geneva accords aimed at the continued development of the individual countries in Southeast Asia and their increasing regional integration—economically, socially and politically. The U.S., through the agency of such programs as the Mekong River Development Scheme and the Asian Development Bank, advocated the concepts of free elections and market economies in Southeast Asia.

President Johnson should have set expectations of the war's costs for the American people. Estimates of the war's duration, casualties and force levels were deliberately avoided. The absence of a consensus among the military and civilian advisors was not an acceptable excuse for his silence on this topic.

General Greene had specifically addressed the potential war costs twice. First in a meeting with members of the House Armed Services Committee (HASC) and then directly to the President in a meeting at the White House. In response to a question from President Lyndon Johnson, Greene stated his estimates in concert with his strategic plan of enclave and civic action: 500,000 U.S. troops, a minimum of five years. Tragically, General Greene's estimates, made before escalation began in 1965, were accurate. The President ignored Greene's advice and counsel, missed an opportunity to inform the American people of the risks and estimates of the costs of war in Southeast Asia, and opted for an attrition strategy. The nation paid the price over the next ten years. The scars of Vietnam - including the absence of lessons learned and the public's reaction to lies from the President - are still with us today.

)( )(

Courageous Dissent

Chapter 3

Strategies
1966

Without debate, without criticism no administration and no country can succeed and no republic can survive. — John F. Kennedy.

Since the end of the Vietnam War in 1975, historians have criticized the U.S. Armed Forces' strategy in Southeast Asia. An excellent critical review was written by Ismaël Fournier, PhD in his paper "Hybrid Warfare in Vietnam." Fournier describes the critiques of various distinguished military historians including John A. Nagl, Andrew F. Krepinevich, Lewis Sorley, Max Boot and others. We chose a more focused approach to judge dissent in years 1965 to 1969. What was the U.S. armed forces strategy, and how did it change? Jack Shulimson, a Marine History Division historian wrote:

> The real war was among the people and not in the mountains. After the Tet offensive in 1968, the U.S. war-fighting effort focused on reoccupying the country. Later, the emphasis shifted to strengthening the territorial forces to free the regular South Vietnamese Army for border protection and other duties.

Specifically, in this chapter, we analyze three pacification strategies (CAP, PROVN and CORDS) and four warfighting strategies (security, enclave, attrition and "one war"), seven in total, and describe the 1966 effort to appraise and dissent one of them.

Retrospective Evaluations of Early Strategies: Marines, Army, and ARVN.

Marine General Lewis Walt, the Marine Commanding General in Vietnam, did not consider the ink blot strategy with its gradual extension of the Marine coastal enclaves as to be necessarily in conflict with General Westmoreland's advocacy of his attrition strategy, his "search and destroy" operations aimed at the enemy main force units. General Walt's position was "Yes, I will engage the enemy's main force units, but first I want to have good intelligence. "

General Victor Krulak viewed the Marine differences with MACV as being more basic. He differed with General Westmoreland "not in a limited way, but in a profound way." Krulak commented in 1978 that his "balanced approach" was a compromise with Westmoreland, and not a balance, and that every man we put into hunting for the NVA was wasted. He sought to persuade his boss Admiral Sharp, Pacific Forces Commander, that "such a compromise would bleed ourselves—and it did."

General Wallace Greene perceived the disagreement between the Marines and MACV in much the same way as General Krulak. General Greene later stated that General Westmoreland and his commanders were preoccupied with the large unit war and that, "From the very beginning the prime error had been the failure to make the population secure—to stamp out the VC hidden in town and hamlet…" I Corps was ideally established geographically (the bulk of the population in a narrow coastal strip) to do this— and to initiate security operations from the sea against key points along the coast. He declared that he had advocated such a strategy in a presentation to the Joint Chiefs and to General Westmoreland. The Chiefs were interested, but Westmoreland wasn't and being Commanding General MACV his views of the big picture prevailed.

Edward Nevgloski, a retired Marine Colonel and future director of the U.S. Marine War College, described the differences between Army and Marine approaches in his PhD dissertation: In *Strange War, Strange Strategy*, he wrote "General Lewis Walt explains that the real war was indeed 'in the rice paddies—in and among the people, not passing through, but living among them night and day—a journey with them towards a better life long overdue'." In other words, pacification was the day-to-day fight and a chief determining factor in winning or losing the long war. That the Marine Corps' leadership doggedly resisted attrition or search and destroy alone was not a rejection of the conventional military threat. Greene, Krulak, and Walt believed that civic actions and CAP would in the long term adversely impact North Vietnamese forces who, in turn, would have to either give battle or wither away." Krulak explained as much in his monthly operation reports to Greene. He supported his position with a cardinal counterinsurgency principle. That principle maintains that

Strategies

Lt. Gen.Krulak shown briefing President Lyndon Johnson in the White House Oval Room. He was a strategic visionary and authored the epic chronicle First to Fight—required reading for all Marines.

if local forces do not move in behind the offensive effort, then the first line forces must be diverted to provide the essential hamlet security, police, and stabilization. From the start, Westmoreland vetoed emphasizing any strategy aimed at disrupting the guerrilla's control of the enclaves at the expense of engaging the main forces and NVA.

Aaron O'Connell, an historian at the Marine War College, reviewed Gregory Daddis' book *Withdrawal: Reassessing America's Final Years in Vietnam*, and summarized their dispute as follows: "the Army and Marines recognized the importance of conducting both types of warfare simultaneously. Disagreements... were not really a debate about strategy, but over priorities in a resource-constrained environment."

The Army of South Vietnam (ARVN) General Ngo Quang Truong was a very highly regarded general officer. He said that CAP units placed in a given village enabled village officials to safely stay in their homes at night and people to live without fear of enemy reprisals. This dynamic developed by CAP units contributed to a significant enhancement of the credibility and the stability of Government of South Vietnam. Also, CAP contributed to the improvement of the South Vietnamese ability to resist the insurgent. Proficiency and combat effectiveness of ARVN soldiers, according to Truong, was directly increased by the Combined Action Program. Sustained presence and amicable relations were crucial to this element of CAP's effectiveness. Only through a mutually agreeable relationship developed through the consistent involvement with the South Vietnamese people would this kind of direct enhancement of stability be possible. The Hamlet Evaluation System (HES), a monthly statistical report that assessed the progress of pacification in South Vietnamese villages, indicated that by 1967 CAP-inhabited hamlets demonstrated nearly twice the advance in security ratings experienced by non-CAP hamlets in I Corps. According to the HES, no CAP inhabited hamlet ever returned to Viet Cong control. Villages inhabited by CAP achieved a 50% higher HES rating than non-CAP villages.

General Westmoreland had a different perspective. He contended that the introduction of North Vietnamese Army units into the South created an entirely new situation. The MACV commander's opinion was that the Communists wanted to develop multi-division forces in relatively secure base areas, while at the same time continuing extensive guerrilla action to tie down allied forces. His intelligence staff section stated that the enemy planned to mount out offensives in 1966 in the provinces northwest of Saigon and in the Central Highlands. The MACV campaign plan for 1966 directed American forces to secure their base areas and to conduct operations in safe havens, areas, and bases. General Walt's III Marine Amphibious Force (MAF) 1966 campaign plan maintained a balance among mutually supporting activities. This "balanced approach" consisted of a three-pronged effort comprised of search and destroy missions, counter guerrilla operations, and pacification.

Adopting the enclave strategy—including the Marine's ink blot concept—would likely have caused the city of Hue to be subsumed within the Phu Bai Marine Tactical Area of Responsibility (TAOR) perimeter. The fight to liberate Hue two years later and the destruction of the ancient imperial and cultural capital of Vietnam, and Walter Cronkite's famous broadcast regarding the "stalemate" of Vietnam would have would likely have been prevented. If General Krulak's rationale in his "Strategic Appraisal - Vietnam" had been followed, the outcome of the Vietnam war might have changed.

Early Pacification Strategies: CAP, PROVN and CORDS

The Combined Action Program (CAP) was developed and implemented by the Marines in 1966. CAP placed squads of Marines into various villages and hamlets in the northern sector of South Vietnam to combat the insurgency in conjunction with Popular Forces South Vietnamese militias. The Popular Force

Platoons (PFP) were recruited from the area where the CAPs were deployed.

Each CAP included a Navy corpsman, a Popular Force Platoon of about 35 men, and a United States Marine rifle squad led by a Marine sergeant. PFPs were usually poorly equipped and trained; they were however knowledgeable and familiar with the local people. The Marines brought with them greater firepower, training, communication with larger units, medical evacuation capabilities and leadership. During the day, the Marines would rest, or train the PFP. At night, patrolling occurred while ambushes with fire power were kept to a minimum. The CAP plan was for the squad to stay in the village for six months and foster familiarity with the locals. CAPs were placed in the five northern districts of Quang Tri: Thien-Hue, Quang Nam Quang Tin and Quang Tai. By 1970, 2500 Marines were involved in CAPs, 114 platoons organized into 20 companies providing security for approximately 135,000 villagers. Overall, CAP service was more dangerous for the Marines. Still, the 1.5 percent of Marines in Vietnam that served in the CAP program would account for eight percent of all enemy casualties.

CAP's strengths included the sustained presence and interaction of the Marines with the local Vietnamese population. The Vietnamese PFPs and the Marines lived among the people. The Marines favored small, mobile, aggressive, and independent patrols freed of logistic constraint, enabling them to hunt down guerrilla units during the night. Long-range patrols enabled the Marines to gain intelligence on the movements of large insurgent forces near populated areas. The majority of Marines in CAP units voluntarily extended the length of their tour to stay with the program. Most South Vietnamese populations felt favorably about the Marines in CAP units. Marines were assigned to CAP units on a voluntary basis. Requirements for consideration included six months of combat experience, above average test scores, and completion of a two-week school covering basic infantry tactics and Vietnamese culture.

CAP's weaknesses included the practical, strategic, and bureaucratic restrictions on personnel. The language barrier also was a major weakness of the CAP program. The expansion of the pacification effort was impeded by the constant redeployment of Marines to the border to meet the conventional threat posed by the NVA. There also were organizational pressures against CAP. The United States Military Assistance Command,

Courageous Dissent

Vietnam (MACV) headquarters favored a war of attrition and fought the concept of CAP from the start. CAP units were not pursued countrywide due to manpower considerations. CAP would never be fully exploited, ending when the Marines began their withdrawal from Vietnam.

Program for the Pacification and Long-Term Development of South Vietnam (PROVN) was designed by The U.S. Army. Chief of Staff General Johnson formed the PROVN team to devise an approach for fighting the war in Vietnam. The PROVN study group began in August 1965 and completed their 900-page report in March 1966. The PROVN summary statement:

> Victory can only be achieved through bringing the individual Vietnamese, typically a rural peasant, to support willingly the Government of South Vietnam (GVN). The critical actions are those that occur at the village, district and provincial levels. This is where the war must be fought; this is where that war and the object which lies beyond it must be won…The U.S. must devise an effective counter to "wars of national liberation."….The proposed U.S. concept of operations is a broad-front offensive which directs major efforts along three mutually supporting axes—eliminating armed Communists; ensuring the effective performance of the GVN; and conducting an effective combined US–GVN Rural Construction Program…The establishment of Rural Construction is the essential vehicle for extending security to, developing the requisite leadership of, and providing the necessary social reform for the Vietnamese people. The war has to be won from the ground up; the people of the countryside are the target. RVNAF must be the main Allied military element supporting Rural Construction, with the U.S. providing material and technical assistance and stimulating social reform as required. Requisite authority and resources must be provided to the province chief.

Secretary McNamara was informed that the Joint Chiefs of Staff did not endorse PROVN in August 1966, and regrettably PROVN was never implemented.

The Office of Civil Operations and Rural Support (CORDS) was organized in May 1967. It was responsible for providing military and civil support of pacification in Vietnam, reporting to the MACV Commander. CORDS included the military, paramilitary, political, economic, and social processes to establish a government that the Vietnamese people would support, coordinating all civil aspects of pacification and development. CORDS was also responsible for the neutralization of the

Viet Cong infrastructure, and provided day-to-day staff direction, training, coordination, and support to field operations. CORDS was the key American program for advising the South Vietnamese on virtually all aspects of life in the countryside, from security to economic, social, and political measures. In February 1968, following the TET offensive, CORDS focused on restoring Government control and, in effect, reoccupying the country. Robert Colby, a former CIA officer and the director of CORDS in 1968, was working closely with the South Vietnamese to develop an effective program, Phoenix, to root out the enemy's underground political apparatus. Later, CORDS' emphasis shifted to strengthening the territorial South Vietnamese forces to concentrate on border protection and other duties.

Robert Komer was a former CIA official and White House aide and the founding Director of CORDS. In a September 1966 letter to Secretary McNamara, Komer stated: "While I'm still only a 5-month expert, I have spent this time 100% on Vietnam.... Most of my ideas have been borrowed liberally from the people and studies which impressed me—especially the PROVN Study... and Brute Krulak."

Early Warfighting Strategies: security, enclave, attrition and "one war"

A security strategy was formed during a National Security Council (NSC) meeting in April 1965 to get United States' combat units involved in the war in Vietnam. The idea was to increase the security of U.S. bases. All nine of the U.S. battalions deployed to Vietnam by June 1965 had base security as their primary mission. Then, President Johnson decided to change the military mission from defense to offense. The Pentagon Papers' historians said this decision made the strategy of base security a "dead letter."

The enclave strategy replaced the security strategy approximately one month later. First presented by Ambassador Maxwell Taylor, it was a way to get U.S. troops engaged at relatively low risk and was implicitly endorsed by President Johnson. It proposed that U.S. troops occupy coastal enclaves, provide full responsibility for enclave security, and be prepared to move as far as 50 miles outside the enclave to go to the rescue of South Vietnam forces. The key to the enclave strategy was to be able to outlast the enemy at the lowest cost to the United States. At first, the

United States experimented with four Marine battalions to see if the concept was feasible.

In the early years 1965-1966, the Marine Corps was responsible for three enclaves in I Corps: Da Nang (530 sq. mi), Chu Lai (205 sq. mi), and Phu Bai (76 sq. mi). The Marine enclaves excluded the city of Hue, headquarters of the 1st Army of the Republic of Vietnam (ARVN) Division, located eight miles north of the Phu Bai enclave. In April 1965, a National Security Memorandum (NSAM 328) marked the beginning of the enclave strategy. The Marine Corps preferred an "ink blot" strategy to aggregate the coastal enclaves, gradually extending U.S. and Vietnamese government control like a spreading inkblot. It was a slow, painstaking process, and both General Westmoreland and Secretary McNamara believed that we did not have sufficient time to implement this strategy. McNamara told General Krulak in the winter of 1965, "A good idea, but too slow." General Krulak believed there was not time to do it any other way but failed to convince either of them. The inkblot strategy was never formally approved.

Instead, the search and destroy or attrition strategy was proposed by General Westmoreland in the early summer of 1965 in an attempt to seize the initiative from the enemy. The basic idea behind search and destroy was the desire to deny the enemy freedom of movement anywhere in the country, taking advantage of the superior firepower and maneuverability of the American and allied forces to deal the heaviest possible blows. The South Vietnamese military would be free to concentrate their efforts in populated areas. It was given presidential sanction in July 1965, when President Johnston accepted General Westmoreland's recommendation for 44 combat battalions, endorsing search-and-destroy and effectively ending the enclave strategy. The military commitment to Vietnam became "open ended".

Marine General Krulak's 1965 appraisal ran the numbers on attrition and demonstrated the futility of that approach, also making two basic points:

> First, no military strategy will promise success unless it gives full discount to the non-military factors of politics, economics, and sociology. And second, manpower being the enemy's area of greatest strength, we have no license and less reason to join battle with him on that ground. The changes in thrust proposed herein are designed around the conviction that scrupulous attention to these two facts is a design for victory, and evasion of their implications is the route to defeat.

Army General Creighton Abrams would assume command of MACV in July 1968 and put in place his "one war" strategy of integrating the political, security, social, and economic aspects of the war with the military resources. Abrams believed he was fighting "a better war" in which the United States and South Vietnamese were creating the conditions necessary for the government of Vietnam's survival long after American forces were gone. His policy was essentially like the Marines' CAP and enclave concepts. This approach would serve as an umbrella for the Marines high mobility strategies of 1968 and 1969.

Presidential Briefings

In Jan 1966, Lt Gen. Victor Krulak was on a quest that would take him to the Oval Office in the White House eight months later. He had served as the Commanding General, Fleet Marine Force Pacific for the past two years, and previously as President Kennedy's Special Assistant for Counterinsurgency and Special Activities (SACSA). Krulak's friendship with President Kennedy had begun nearly 20 years earlier during WW II in the Solomon Islands Campaign. Members of Krulak's battalion were cut off on a hostile beach during the Bougainville Operation and radioed for help. Ensign John Kennedy's PT boat answered the call. Years later, to return the favor, Krulak delivered a gift of Three Feathers Whiskey to the new President.

In his role as SACSA, Krulak would meet with President Kennedy ten times on the topic of Vietnam. One of his last assignments from Kennedy came when McNamara sent Krulak to Vietnam on a fact-finding trip. Ambassador Harriman insisted on sending senior Foreign Service officer Joseph Mendenhall to accompany Krulak. After three days, Krulak and Mendenhall returned, with opposite reports from their visit. Krulak optimistically described the SVN army as willing to fight, patriotic and reliable. Mendenhall described the SVN military as unreliable, immersed in politics and likely to defect, prompting President Kennedy to ask Mendenhall and Krulak: "Have you two gentlemen been to the same country?"

Krulak was deeply concerned about the U.S. policy in Vietnam and wrote a paper "A Strategic Appraisal-Vietnam" to frame both strategies: pacification and war fighting. He met with Secretary McNamara to discuss "Appraisal" and was referred to meet with Ambassador Averell Harriman. Harriman invited Krulak to lunch at 3038 N Street in Georgetown, one of the most famous houses in Washington. Harriman had lived there for years, except for a brief time in late 1963 when the house was offered to Jackie Kennedy and her children, following the assassination of President Kennedy. Harriman was one of the most experienced diplomats in the Johnson administration. A 1913 Yale graduate, he inherited the largest fortune in America and became Yale's youngest crew coach. A 1934 Annapolis graduate, Krulak was paid $124 a month and became Navy's shortest crew coach. However, rowing was not discussed that day.

Following their luncheon, Harriman invited Krulak to present his strategic plan for achieving victory in Vietnam. When Krulak arrived at the climax of the plan, which recommended striking North Vietnam to "destroy the port areas, mine the ports, destroy the rail lines, destroy power, fuel, and heavy industry," Harriman stopped him and demanded, "Do you want a war with the Soviet Union or the Chinese?" Krulak later wrote, "I winced when I thought about the kind of advice he was giving President Johnson and Secretary Dean Rusk." Secretary McNamara had been impressed with Krulak's statistical approach but did not follow up to arrange a meeting with the President. Krulak was not successful, but he did not give up. He informed his boss, and General Greene made the call to the White House.

Krulak was invited to meet in the Oval Office on 1 August 1966 to discuss the same strategic plan. LBJ's first question was "What is it going to take to win?" Krulak responded: "Improve the quality of the South Vietnamese government, accelerate the training of the SVN forces, stop the flow of war materials to the North Vietnamese army, mine the ports, destroy the Haiphong dock area." When Krulak switched from discussing pacification to mining the ports, President Johnson "Looked like he sat on tack... got to his feet, put his arm around my shoulder, and propelled me firmly toward the door." Nearly two years later on 26 April 1968, President Johnson nominated Lt Gen. Krulak for appointment to the retired list. His 34-year Marine career was over. In the next three years, a total of seven war fighting strategies and pacification plans were developed and evaluated. Following the TET offensive 1968, the "one war" strategy integrated military and non-military activities for the first time—three years after the Marines had landed.

)○(

Strategies

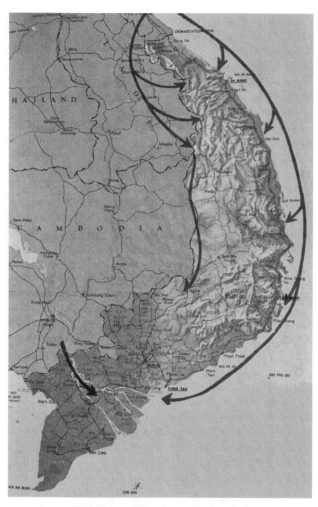

*North Vietnam infiltration routes along South
Vietnam coastline and the western borders with Laos and Cambodia*

Courageous Dissent

Chapter 4

The Barrier
1967

War is the unfolding of miscalculations. —Barbara Tuchman

On 14 October 1966, the last day of his Vietnam trip, the Secretary of Defense was exhausted. After four long days, he settled into his seat on the windowless KC-135 jet outfitted for long-distance VIP travel for the trip home. The airplane was named after him: "The McNamara Special." His primary aims for the trip were (1) completing his plan to build a high-tech, anti-infiltration barrier across the DMZ and (2) fact finding to justify denying the latest request from the Military Assistance Command (MACV) for more troops. Sadly, he succeeded with the first aim, and failed with the second. The eastern section of the barrier system would be built and often referred to as The McNamara Line. More troops would be added.

The trip was not a happy one, another episode in an unhappy year. The war was going badly, and McNamara's views were changing—from hawk to dove. His Vietnam visit began at the Saigon Embassy where he made clear his deep dissatisfaction with the slow progress of pacification. He told Ambassador Henry Cabot Lodge that the current organization was incompetent, and that the State Department lacked the abilities to handle a program of the size and complexity of nation building in South Vietnam. The following days were easier—meetings with a variety of U.S. government officials and South Vietnamese leaders, and with General William Westmoreland, the Commander in Vietnam. At Saigon headquarters multiple briefing officers delivered optimistic reports inflating the war's progress. McNamara's views about the war had changed, and he reacted pessimistically to the briefings. He was, however, more hopeful about the discussion of the proposed barrier. After the briefing, he announced "I will absolutely guarantee that a year from today there is going to be a barrier up there." The senior briefing officer, a colonel (and future Army general) summed it up: "Mc-

Namara struck me as a fool, however intelligent he obviously was."

The last day of McNamara's trip began at Da Nang Airbase with a big meeting at III MAF Marine headquarters, the Barrier Conference. The VIP list showed 14 attendees, including Secretary McNamara, Under Secretary of State Katzenbach, General Westmoreland, Chairman of the Joint Chiefs of Staff General Wheeler, and others. McNamara and Westmoreland flew by helicopter along the DMZ, and to Khe Sanh, viewing the terrain for a proposed L-shaped barrier. Westmoreland described his own version of the barrier plan: fewer hi-tech sensors and mines, and more reinforced bunkers in "strong point" forts, backed up by air power and artillery. Secretary McNamara agreed to General Westmoreland's changes. The barrier would be built, despite an initial price tag of $1B, lack of support from the Joint Chiefs, and the objections of the Marines who would eventually be ordered to build and defend it. Years later, the total cost of the barrier — including construction, multiple specialized aircraft, computers, and sensors that would be used in Laos— would be estimated as high as $6 billion.

McNamara's trip had begun the previous week in mid-October of 1966 when the KC-135 had lifted off from Andrews Air Base bound for Saigon. The Secretary was seated in the non-sleeping section, at a table with his deputy John McNaughton. Across the aisle was a briefing officer with a briefcase full of memos he had written on the topic of Vietnam. Almost immediately, the briefing officer opened his briefcase and began passing McNaughton and McNamara 200 pages of memos, which described his views and experiences in the State Department and as a Marine Captain in Vietnam. McNamara read all the memos. They were overwhelmingly negative, helping to remove McNamara's remaining illusions about the progress of the conflict in Vietnam. The noisy KC-135 flight meeting could have been held in Cambridge, MA—inside the staid red bricks of the Harvard faculty club. McNamara and McNaughton had both taught at Harvard Business & Law Schools, and the original barrier proposal was written by Roger Fisher also of Harvard. The briefing officer had been a PhD student at Harvard's School of Arts & Sciences, where Dr. Henry Kissinger was his favorite professor. The briefing officer's name was Daniel Ellsberg.

On the Monday after returning from Vietnam, Secretary McNamara sent his report to the President. "I see no reasonable

Barrier

Members of 3rd Platoon, Company A, 3rd Reconnaissance Battalion, led by 1stLt Theard J. Terrebonne, Jr., at Dong Ha after a patrol extraction in July 1966. During this period, 14 out of 18 patrols in the DMZ sector had to be withdrawn because of enemy contact. (Marine Corps Photo A332831)

way to bring the war to an end soon... We find ourselves no better, and if anything, worse off." The President approved both the barrier plan, assigning it "the highest national priority," and Westmoreland's request to escalate the war. Khe Sanh was named as the western terminus of the barrier. One month later, in a real faculty meeting at Harvard University's Institute of Politics in Cambridge, MA, the idea occurred to McNamara to commission a study that would trace the history of the United States political and military involvement in Vietnam from 1945 to 1967. The official title of the study was "Report of the Office of the Secretary of Defense Vietnam Task Force." Daniel Ellsberg would release the study in June 1971 to the New York Times where it was dubbed *The Pentagon Papers*.

The War in the North — NVA Infiltration

In 1966, Hanoi sent the NVA 324B Division across the Demilitarized Zone (DMZ) into Quang Tri province in South Vietnam. The first indication of the NVA 324B Division was seen by a United States Marine patrol, led by First Lieutenant Theard J. Terrebonne, Jr. The patrol was participating in Operation Hastings, the largest operation of the U.S. Marines in the war. Terrebonne's platoon moved into the area 16 miles west of Dong Ha where a 700-foot mountain known as the Rockpile dominated the landscape.

During the 24-hour period that the patrol remained in the vicinity of the Rockpile, they observed several well-camouflaged enemy firing positions including trench lines, mortar pits, and fighting holes. The reconnaissance Marines sighted more than 300 NVA troops. Two days later, 1st ARVN Division troops captured a NVA soldier near the Rockpile. He identified his unit as part of the 5th Battalion, 812th Regiment of the 324B Division and stated that the other regiments of the division, the 90th and the 803d, also had entered South Vietnam.

NVA Artillery - 1966, 1967

The use of long-range NVA artillery had become more common in 1966. The 122 mm howitzer, 130 mm gun, and the 152 mm gun-howitzer significantly increased NVA fire power for attacking logistic facilities and supporting infantry operations. The U.S. response to NVA operations was to employ more firepower, and the NVA suffered horribly. However, Westmoreland did not send troops north after the NVA attacks, and Hanoi could expect the U.S. to operate in a defensive/reactive posture. The threat of a U.S. invasion of North Vietnam was small.

Soviet and Chinese Communist rockets were added to the NVA inventory. When compared to tube artillery, rockets were not only more suitable for attacking larger targets, but also lighter and more adaptable. And because of their low trajectory, rockets often escaped location by the U.S. counter-mortar radar. The 140-mm rocket attack on Da Nang air base commenced a new phase in the war by extending the NVA attack range by 3,500 yards beyond the maximum range of the 120-mm mortar, more than doubling the warhead payload. Moreover, rockets were more mobile than conventional artillery.

In February 1967, along the DMZ, NVA units, for the first time, defended key terrain from well-constructed, fortified lines. In July 1967, NVA artillery scored a direct hit on the command bunker of the 1st Battalion, 9th Marines at Con Thien. A 152 - mm howitzer round, penetrated five feet of sandbags, loose dirt, and 12x12-inch timbers. The same day, at Dong Ha, a delay-fused 130 - mm round landed at the base of the North wall of the 9th Marines' command post, exploding six feet below the bunker floor. The NVA also scored a direct hit on the Dong Ha chapel during Catholic services, killing the chaplain's assistant.

Barrier

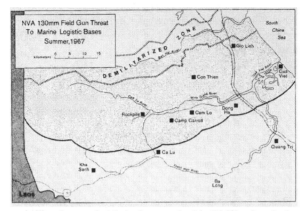

Artillery threat to the Marine bases south of the DMZ and north of road 9. Max 130mm Field Gun Range: 31,000 meters. Range fan is measured from the north bank of the Ben Hai River.

Storage areas, helicopter maintenance areas, and medical facilities were among the targets of the NVA long-range weapons. During that July in Operation Buffalo, NVA artillery accounted for half of the Marine casualties and posed a constant threat to the Marine logistical support installations. In August, Dong Ha experienced three separate attacks; 150 rocket and artillery rounds destroyed two helicopters and damaged 24 others. Forty-one artillery rounds slammed into Dong Ha base, destroying the ammunition storage area and bulk fuel farm and damaging 17 helicopters. To prevent future attacks, III Marine Amphibious Force moved the logistics base from Dong Ha south to Quang Tri, beyond the range of the enemy's 130 mm guns.

The Barrier Concept

In January 1966, Roger Fisher, a consultant with the U.S. Department of Defense, wrote a memo to his friend John McNaughton, Secretary Robert McNamara's assistant. He was suggesting that a 160-mile barrier be built across Vietnam and Laos consisting of minefields, barbed wire, ditches, and military strong points (fixed positions) flanked by a defoliated strip on each side, and an air-dropped line of conventional obstacles intended to inhibit the flow of troops and supplies from the North. The purpose of Fisher's proposal was to provide the Administration with an alternative strategic concept for arresting infiltration, thereby permitting a cessation of the bombing that was failing to break Hanoi's will. If the barrier could stop the infiltration, the bombing of North Vietnam could be stopped, too.

Fisher already had extensive experience working with the military. During World War II, he served in the U.S. Army Air Force in the North Atlantic and Pacific as a weather reconnaissance observer. After discovering that his college roommate and two of his best friends were killed in the war, he dedicated most of his life to finding a better way to deal with the kind of differences that produce war. Fisher taught at the Naval War College, Air War College, the NATO Defense College, and at West Point, training Army officers and cadets to apply the tools of principled negotiation in peace and war. In the 1960s, Fisher served as a consultant to John McNaughton, Assistant U.S. Secretary of Defense for International Security Affairs. McNaughton, like Fisher a former Harvard Law School professor, was the key advisor to Secretary Robert McNamara. Later, Fisher co-founded the Harvard Negotiation Project, establishing negotiation and conflict resolution as an academic study, and devoted his teaching career to alternative methods of dispute resolution. His accomplishments are impressive: peace in the Middle East, including Sadat's trip to Jerusalem and the Camp David summit, peace in Central America - especially in El Salvador, the breakthrough that enabled resolution of the 1980 Iranian hostage conflict, reshaping the U.S.-Soviet relationship; and the negotiations that ended apartheid in South Africa. His best-selling book, *Getting to Yes: Negotiating Without Giving In*, would eventually sell more than 4 million copies worldwide, and has been translated into 23 languages.

The idea behind the barrier strategy was to prevent attacks, which was an alternative to being compelled to retaliate after being attacked. "There is," said Fisher, "a difference between physically preventing action versus trying to influence it by increasing costs…a difference between influence and physical effect… preventing versus inflicting pain." Fisher was not thinking about sit-down negotiations such as we might with the Russians. Rather, he advocated to let our actions speak loudly. If the barrier could stop the infiltration, the bombing of North Vietnam could be stopped, too. Fisher had worked directly for Averell Harriman and was undoubtedly aware of the Geneva Accords prohibition against military forces in Laos; his military experience in France guaranteed that he knew of the Maginot Line failure in WWII.

Fisher's memo struck a responsive chord in McNaughton. Six weeks after receiving it, he sent McNamara an only slightly revised version of the Fisher draft. For an option-oriented policy adviser like McNamara, the task was to find alternative ways of accomplishing the job. The idea of constructing an anti-infiltration barrier across the DMZ and the Laotian panhandle was a plausible alternative to the bombing of North Vietnam. He agreed with the concept, ignored any advice to the contrary, approved the barrier project and never looked back. The barrier would tragically become a colossal failure.

JASON was an independent consulting group of distinguished scientists organized by the Pentagon to advise the government on scientific matters. They began in 1960 with approximately 30 members and doubled in size within the next few years. Six months following Fisher's memo, the JASON's wrote a report expanding the concept into a detailed barrier plan. Most of the JASON's work was highly classified, and their reports - however influential - were kept secret. They met in the summer of 1966 with a similar group of scientists called JASON EAST at Dana Hall School in Wellesley, MA, also in secret. Several reports were developed and then published in August 1966 as a result of that collaboration, including "Air-Supported Anti-Infiltration Barrier" and "Air-Sown Mines for the Massive Barrier."

The purpose of the barrier strategy was to reduce infiltration by interdicting movement on the Ho Chi Minh Trail. Relying more on technology than large troop commitments, the barrier plan was to install an electronic fence, supplemented by mines and air-ground surveillance. This barrier would extend across South Vietnam just south of the Demilitarized Zone (DMZ) and south into Laos. Originally a single concept, the barrier evolved into two distinct parts, each "owned" by different military services. *Dye Marker* was the name of an L-shaped barrier consisting of strong points, fixed positions including Con Thien, Gio Linh, Cam Lo and C2, located east-west along the DMZ, and then south to Khe Sanh. *Dye Marker* was owned by the 3rd Marine Division. *Muscle Shoals* was the name of the electronic sensors forming an electronic barrier along the Ho Chi Minh Trail located in Laos. *Igloo White* was the name of the common technology framework for both parts of the barrier. *Muscle Shoals* and *Igloo White* were owned by the 7th Air Force.

Courageous Dissent

The Barrier Conference

In October 1966, the week following McNamara's Vietnam trip, the barrier conference would be held, also in Da Nang. A summary of that meeting was recorded in hand-written notes by Lt Col Morrison of the 3rd Marine Division. His notes reveal more questions than answers: what were the roles of the 1st ARVN division (6,000 troops), the participation of a Korean division (12,000 troops), and major port developments at Dong Ha? His notes also included an important observation—the barrier plan would commit major forces that could not leave the DMZ area to respond to the NVA's predictable end run of the barrier. Major General Wood Kyle, Commanding General of the 3rd Marine Division would be named the barrier "owner," also asked questions about command and control, construction costs, and the increased logistical needs. Good questions; no answers.

The eastern part of the barrier was strongly opposed by the Marine Corps. From the plan's inception, the Marine generals complained that the system would tie down their troops in fixed positions and reduce their ability to defeat enemy infiltration through the DMZ. At General Westmoreland's direction, the Marines proceeded with barrier planning but expressions of unhappiness with the project were heard at every level of the Marine chain of command. The western part of the barrier (*Igloo White*) was implemented by the Air Force, with albeit mixed results over the life of the barrier. The overall technology program included three components: (1) sensors, including the Air-Delivered Seismic Intrusion Detector (ADSID). This was the most widely used sensor in the program, designed for use on the Ho Chi Minh Trail in Laos and at Khe Sanh; (2) orbiting aircraft to relay the sensor signals, a variant of the Lockheed Constellation airliner (EC 121), followed by a much smaller single engine plane (QU-22); and (3) *Dutch Mill*, the barrier nerve center, also known as Task Force Alpha, which was built in late 1967 and located in Nakhon Phanom Thailand (NKP).

Muscle Shoals operations on the Ho Chi Minh trail would not begin until early 1968, slowed considerably in 1972, and stopped altogether in 1973 when the IBM 325 computers at NKP were packed up and shipped home to the United States. In March 1973, the 7th Air Force left Saigon and moved to NKP, occupied the Task Force Alpha building for two years, and deactivated it in June 1975. *Dye Marker* lasted for one year, *Muscle Shoals* sur-

Barrier

Marine Major General Wood Kyle, then Commanding General, Third Maine Division, with General Westmoreland

vived for five years. Ironically, the Air Force and the Marines had been the two services most opposed to McNamara's idea to begin with and yet ended up as "owners" of the barrier.

The 1966 barrier conference was a formal opportunity for the Marines to express their opposition to this concept. That dissent was clearly expressed in a three-page report (Appendix C), signed by General Kyle, the Commanding General and designated "owner" of the eastern portion of the barrier. Titled *Nonconcur*, the report was a reply to the plan presented by the Saigon Headquarters, MACV. Their barrier implementation plan was titled *Concept for Conduct of Defensive Operations in the Vicinity of the DMZ* and was presented at the barrier conference. Major General Kyle's report was summarized as follows: "The barrier defense system should free Marine forces for operations elsewhere, not freeze such forces in a barrier-watching defensive role. When the additional forces to maintain the defile barriers and connect-

Courageous Dissent

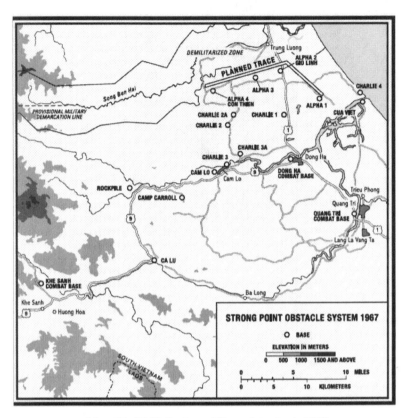

Map of the DMZ, Barrier, and Strongpoint system in 1967.

ing roads are considered...a mobile and flexible defense by two divisions would be more efficient and cost effective than the participation of like forces in conjunction with a barrier system." Within the next three months, the Marine's objection was repeated to two visitors from Washington: General Wallace Greene, the Commandant of the Marine Corps, and Robert Baldwin, the Undersecretary of the Navy.

To make matters worse, the original MACV plan included one division of Korean troops, and a second group of ARVN troops to be stationed along the DMZ. However, neither was included in the eventual plan, and the 3rd Marine Division had to "make-do." In addition to constructing and defending the barrier, Marine headquarters had to add additional troops to defend Khe Sanh. The Marines' *Non-concur* memo was ignored, and the *Dye Marker* barrier was built and then abandoned one year later.

Barrier Construction

In March 1967, both the NVA artillery and the NVA 324B Division were big trouble and were now joined with a third problem - the barrier. The Marines accepted reality and began construction work. Combat engineers began clearing a "trace" along the DMZ. In September 1967, Defense Secretary Robert S. McNamara called a press conference and announced that the United States would build a complex barrier between North and South Vietnam in hopes of hindering enemy infiltration. Confirming the widely published reports that the United States planned such a barrier, he declined to give any details of how it would work other than to say that equipment to be installed would range from barbed wire to highly sophisticated devices. Secretary McNamara also would not say how far the barrier would extend along the Demilitarized Zone.

The first step in building the barrier amounted to bulldozing a strip 600 yards wide and about six miles long from Gio Linh near the coast toward Con Thien to the West. Initially, wooden watch towers were erected and were promptly burned down by the enemy. The barrier Mr. McNamara talked about would be a new strip stretching eastward 15 miles toward Laos.

Two weeks later, Assistant Secretary of Defense Paul Warnke recommended to Secretary McNamara that the Joint Chiefs examine the feasibility of moving the manned portion of the barrier system 10–15 kilometers farther south beyond the range of the NVA 130mm guns to reduce artillery casualties and improve tactical flexibility. Secretary McNamara wrote on the margins of Warnke's memo to him, "Disinclined to start such a study now." McNamara forged ahead with the barrier project over the protests of military leaders, who contended it would not be worth the effort. The military leaders dissented claiming it would take an inordinate number of troops to make the barrier effective. They would rather have more troops to step up the ground war in South Vietnam.

In 1999, thirty years later, Marine Major General Metzger wrote an article in the Marine Corps Gazette, describing the negative impact of the barrier decision on the 3rd Marine Division. General Metzger comments on the barrier—its cost and impact on the overall war—can be summarized in the following quote.

> The terrible cost of men and material can never be completely reckoned. Marine Corps history recorded the *Dye Marker* effort and

its associated security had required 757,520 man-days and 114,519 equipment hours by 31 December 1967. Equipment lost to enemy action amounted to a monetary loss of $1,622,348. To this cost must be added the over $16 million spent on construction materials. Not included in that figure is the cost of transporting materials from the United States, then to Da Nang, then to the Cua Vet River, then upriver to Dong Ha. It is impossible to calculate the number of casualties caused by this debacle, as it cannot be determined which are attributable to the Wall and which to combat operations. Needless to say, they were high. There can be no doubt that this ill-planned and ill-conceived project, imposed over the strenuous objection at every level of military command from the field to the Joint Chiefs of Staff, had an adverse impact on the entire Vietnamese War.

NVA Offensive

At the beginning of 1967, as the Marines were constructing the barrier, the NVA in Hanoi was considering strategic shifts. The North Vietnamese were close to deciding on their strategy: choosing between a protracted war, which was the preference of their closest ally, China, or a negotiated settlement, which was the preference of their wealthiest ally, Russia. By the spring of 1967, the NVA would launch an offensive in the hills around Khe Sanh and the 1968 Tet offensive would begin eight months later. Neither the Military Assistance Command, Vietnam (MACV) headquarters in Saigon, nor the Johnson administration in Washington saw it coming. The U.S. air war strategy was bombing in North Vietnam and Laos; the ground war strategy was a defensive posture in South Vietnam. The Air War, code-named *Rolling Thunder*, had been declared a failure in a report written by JASON in July 1966.

The Hill Fights at Khe Sanh in May 1967 were the first large scale NVA offensive in 1967. Following the Khe Sanh Hill Fights, the NVA launched the first of two attacks against Con Thien, a small U.S. Marine Fire Base located atop a barren hill south of the DMZ. The NVA attacks against Con Thien were reinforced by heavy artillery, rockets, and mortars sited north of the Ben Hai River. Then, a series of bloody engagements fought by the U.S. Army, known as "The Border Battles," followed at Song Be, Loc Ninh and Dak To. In October 1967, the NVA 88th Regiment attacked the ARVN 5th Division at Song Be, and the NVA 273d Regiment attacked the town of Loc Ninh, a pair

Barrier

of American outposts near the Cambodian border north of Saigon.

Central Office for South Vietnam (COSVN) was the North Vietnamese political and military headquarters inside South Vietnam responsible for organizing and directing the communist effort including the Viet Cong. The Loc Ninh battle represented the first time that COSVN had coordinated attacks from different divisions which was intended as a "rehearsal" to experiment with urban-fighting techniques to be used later in the Tet Offensive. COSVN goals were to draw U.S. and ARVN forces away from the cities, in preparation for that offensive.

In July 1967, Hanoi issued Resolution 13, adopting the strategy of the General Offensive, General Uprising (Vietnamese acronym: TCK/TKN). In August 1967, the Central Office of Vietnam (COSVN) discussed the strategy of "fighting while negotiating" at the Front's Third Congress. At the conclusion of the Congress, a new coalition government concept was created to use as a negotiating chip during the next phase of the war. Hanoi hoped the Americans, growing weary of the war, would accept an honorable exit from Vietnam. The North Vietnamese believed that if the Americans would allow the existence of this coalition government, even if existing alongside the current government in Saigon, they would agree to gradually withdraw troops. Hanoi could then avert the strain of the Sino-Soviet dispute and eventually reunify the country on its own timetable.

In November 1967, the NVA began the largest engagement of the Vietnam war to date, around Dak To in the mountains above Pleiku. The U.S. Army's 4th Infantry Division and the 173rd Airborne Brigade did the brunt of the fighting against the NVA First Division. The NVA designed this offensive to again try and draw American and South Vietnamese forces away from the large cities.

Coincidentally, NVA regulars began to mass near Khe Sanh —the NVA 304th Division of Dien Bien Phu fame accompanied by the NVA 320th Division. U.S. intelligence also detected the NVA 325th Division, and a regiment of the NVA 324B division. Again, their main emphasis was to draw American units away from the populated areas in the lowlands. When the U.S. responded, the Viet Cong would infiltrate the coastal urban areas to prepare themselves and the Southern revolution for the General Uprising. At Khe Sanh, the U.S. response was to use more firepower, and the NVA suffered horribly. But Hanoi witnessed again that Westmoreland did not send troops north. Hanoi could expect American forces to continue operating in a defensive/reactive posture. The significance of Khe Sanh is that it allowed Hanoi to order TCK/TKN with the confidence that the U.S. would not counterattack into the North.

General Vo Nguyen Giap, commander in chief of North Vietnam's military forces, had carefully tracked the gradual progression of General Westmoreland's tactics. He was constructing border strong points along infiltration routes where he could both interdict Communist infiltration and launch strikes into Communist base areas across the border when granted permission. Giap knew that Westmoreland's next move, if he had his way, would be beyond the borders of South Vietnam. Giap was correct. General Westmoreland was planning to use fortified border base camps, his "strong point obstacle system," to stage incursions into Laos and North Vietnam. Westmoreland "hoped a new administration in Washington would approve." An operation code named *York* was being planned to sweep into Laos and support a U.S. invasion of North Vietnam. However, The White House never approved Westmoreland's request to invade North Vietnam or Laos, and in November, President Johnson announced that Secretary McNamara would leave government to take a position as President of the World Bank.

Proposal to Interdict the Ho Chi Minh Trail

In November 1967, Major Bob Coolidge, Third Marine Division, G-2 intelligence officer, arranged a meeting with Captain Mirza Baig and Brigadier General Louis Metzger, Third Marine Division Acting Commander. The purpose of the meeting was to review Baig's idea for disrupting North Vietnamese Army (NVA) traffic on the Ho Chi Minh Trail. His proposal was a guerrilla force of Marine commandos that would destroy NVA re-supply convoys, operating undetected behind enemy lines and living off the land. The three officers already knew each other. Coolidge had met Baig several years earlier in California, when Baig made a series of presentations to Marine pilots and sergeants about what to expect in their upcoming deployments to Vietnam. Coolidge was well known to senior Marine officers in the Third Marine Division, having conducted daily intelligence briefings for the Division Commander and his staff.

Captain Baig was both typical and unique as a junior Marine officer. Of Pakistani descent, his father was a prominent diplomat and, with the assistance of the Commandant of the Marine Corps and his green card, Baig enlisted in the Marines in 1957 and was commissioned as a second lieutenant three years later. Baig served two tours in Vietnam. His first tour in 1963-64 was with the 3rd Division Counterintelligence Team, responsible for both civil affairs in a Vietnam village and clandestine activities in North Vietnam. During his second tour in 1967, Captain Baig would first serve as battery commander for the 1st 155 Battery, self-propelled howitzers in Phu Bai. Now Baig was back in intelligence, serving as 3rd Division G-2 clandestine military intelligence coordinator. Baig presented his briefing in meticulous detail. Standing with the large, curved, wide blade of an Indian kukri knife at his side, and stomping his boots like a British officer, he spoke in a clipped British accent, sounding a bit like Basil Rathbone. Baig's proposal for the Ho Chi Minh Trail was never implemented.

Brigadier General Metzger had served as Assistant Division Commander since May 1967. Metzger would serve as the acting Commanding General of the 3rd Marine Division for two weeks in late November, following the death in a helicopter crash of Major General Bruno Hocmuth, who had assumed command after Major General Kyle. Metzger had extensive combat experience in Asia, fighting against the Chinese in Korea and against the Japanese in the Pacific. At age 27, he had commanded a Marine battalion in the battles for Guam and Okinawa, and after the war had written most of the Marine Corps' manual for armored amphibious doctrine. A graduate of Stanford University and former Naval attaché in London, Metzger was known as a knowledgeable and experienced Marine, with a background in military intelligence.

General Metzger had a lot on his mind in 1967. Thirty-seven NVA battalions were operating in the vicinity of the Demilitarized Zone (DMZ), the September 1967 destruction of 18,000 tons of ammunition at the Dong Ha ammunition dump by NVA artillery, the October 1967 grounding of more than 100 CH 46A helicopters, resulting in the loss of half of the Marine airlift capability, and 5,000 Marines killed or wounded around the DMZ. Of all his problems, the worst was building and defending the Strong Points of the anti-infiltration barrier, aka "The McNamara Line". With 130 long range NVA artillery sites located north of the Ben Hai River, his Marines were exposed and vulnerable.

The 15th Marine Counterintelligence Team and U.S. Army intelligence had established electronic collection nets across the Ben Hai River. These nets had penetrated several NVA headquarters and other organizations. One of their tasks was to report the movements of the 4th Battalion, Van An Rocket Artillery Regiment, and the Vinh Linh Rocket Battery together with escorting NVA infantry. Earlier in 1967, these NVA units had caused much damage to the Marine bases at Dong Ha and Cua Viet. Ominously, both NVA units would soon head south to Khe Sanh and participate in the fighting there.

Multiple plans would be proposed by the military to disrupt infiltration from North Vietnam:
- Invading Laos - an "airhead" operation in the Laotian Bolovens plateau, which was a favorite of General Westmoreland, was rejected in 1966.
- A North Vietnam amphibious raid plan — operation *Butt Stroke*, that included the Army, Navy, and Marines, was withdrawn in 1968.
- Two other Laos invasion plans (*El Paso I +II*), were rejected in 1968.
- An anti-infiltration barrier aka "The McNamara Line," a series of defoliated traces and "strong point" fire bases located along the DMZ and south to Khe Sanh.

Only the "McNamara Line" was approved in late 1966, construction began in early 1967, and was stopped by the end of the year. Cost estimates included thousands of U.S. Marine casualties, and six billion dollars. In December 1967, Major General Rathvon M. Tompkins would assume command of the 3rd Division.

※ ※

Chapter 5

Khe Sanh
1968

Nine-tenths of tactics are certain, and taught in books: but the irrational tenth is like the kingfisher flashing across the pool, and that is the test of generals. —*T. E. Lawrence*

In 1966, the management of the Vietnam War was changing. The two key war managers— General Westmoreland and Secretary McNamara—had concluded, for different reasons, that the U.S. strategy was failing. McNamara favored cessation of strategic bombing and a passive defensive approach in the ground war. Westmoreland had begun to recognize the failure of attrition in the ground war and favored invading Laos. For those completely different reasons, the two men ultimately agreed to build the barrier to further their own versions for an alternate strategy to win the Vietnam War. Electronic sensors would be used along the Ho Chi Minh Trail in Laos together with a series of strong points along the Demilitarized Zone (DMZ), aka "The McNamara Line." Khe Sanh was designated as the southern terminus of the barrier and a major strong point to be defended.

On the morning of 20 November 1970, during a hearing before the United States Senate Committee on Armed Services, Marine General Rathvon Tompkins read a letter that he had recently received from Marine Captain Mirza Baig to the assembled Senators. In 1968, Baig had served in the intelligence section of the 26th Marine Regiment defending the Khe Sanh Combat Base (KSCB), when Tompkins was Commanding General of the Third Marine Division. The letter described the siege at Khe Sanh as Baig experienced it. At one point, the General paused dramatically and emphasized "This is Captain Baig speaking."

Everyone in the room knew about Khe Sanh. For 77 days in 1968, the battle was viewed on TV in nearly every American home. According to Peter Braestrup in *Big Story*, Khe Sanh alone accounted for twenty-five percent of the press coverage for the entire 1968 Tet offensive. Baig's letter was compelling and graphic: an explanation of critical tactical information including the raw data from the new hi-tech sensors that had arrived at Khe Sanh before Baig himself, and the rationale for using them for the first time in a combat situation. Baig even described an error he made interpreting the data from the brand-new devices.

The data had been gathered from sensors planted around Khe Sanh. The first devices arrived in Khe Sanh and were installed just two weeks before the first major NVA attack on Khe Sanh Combat Base. The Marines were surprised by the sensors. They had been diverted to Khe Sanh from their intended use on the Ho Chi Minh Trail. Gen. Tomkins explained to the Senators that Baig was the only officer in Khe Sanh who had "some experience" with the sensors. In fact, Baig admitted that he knew very little about their accuracy or reliability. He had first learned of the concept of sensors in 1966, when he briefed the top-secret JASON group that developed the plan for an anti-infiltration barrier.

Following General Tompkins' presentation, Colonel David Lounds spoke next. He had been the commanding officer of the 26th Marine Regiment during the siege at Khe Sanh and explained "the sensor is not a panacea...but is a valuable tool for coordination of firepower... expendable, something that your and my son are not." In the coming years, improved versions of the sensors would contribute to the developing Electronic Battlefield.

Khe Sanh Background

The Third Marine Amphibious Force (III MAF) was responsible for the Khe Sanh area, but Marine war planners felt the better use of their forces was in population centers in the lowlands, conducting operations to protect the Government and commercial activity. They did not see tactical value in holding Khe Sanh and saw problems with any plans for placing a small force at Khe Sanh. They knew that defending the KSCB airfield meant defending the key terrain and the lines of communication, which, along with occupation of the airstrip, would impose personnel demands that III MAF felt they could not afford. Positioning a force large enough to hold KSCB would draw more forces away from the population centers they felt were strategically critical, and impose logistics demands that were out of proportion to the benefits to be gained.

III MAF might have been responsible for the northern part of the country, but Army Special Forces and "irregular" forces under tacit control of the CIA had a tactical headquarters near the Khe Sanh airfield. Occupied since 1962, they operated outside of III MAF control. The airfield at Khe Sanh had been established by the French Army several years earlier for light planes only. In the best location for several kilometers around, it was situated about two kilometers north of Route 9 on a plateau with its long-axis running slightly north of east-west. The terrain surrounding the airfield, which came to be designated as the Khe Sanh Combat Base (KSCB), was dense foliage, except for a roadway just south of the airfield, which ran southeast and connected to Route 9 and the nearby villages of Khe Sanh and Huong Hoa. Huong Hoa was the capital of the Hoang Hoa District of Quang Tri Province.

Route 9 was shown on maps as the northern-most east-west highway south of the Demilitarized Zone (DMZ) that separated north and South Vietnam. As a practical matter, Route 9 was of the French colonial era: a worn and narrow, winding gravel and black-top road, intersected by over 30 bridges. Overgrown, and pot-holed, it was not maintained because it led to nowhere that anyone really cared to go. Route 9 was often cut by enemy activity and incapable of sustaining a serious logistics effort.

Although KSCB was on a plateau, that plateau was dominated militarily by the key terrain in the area, which was a series of hills that effectively placed KSCB in a valley. Hill 950, the tallest of the surrounding hills that were all named by their altitude in meters, was directly to the North (see map). It was a pinnacle that was very small at the crest, about 3.5 km away. Moving 2.3 km west from 950, hill 558 dominated the approach routes from the North, and then 1.5 km to the west-south-west was the next dominant military feature, hill 861. Continuing another 2.5 km was hill 881S (south), and hill 881N (north), about 1.9 km to the north of it. Hill 881S was 7 km from the West end of KSCB, directly along the axis of the runway. More hills continue around the rest of the valley, creating a rough circle, broken only by Route 9 to the East and to the Southwest. And virtually all the terrain between the airfield and the hills was broken

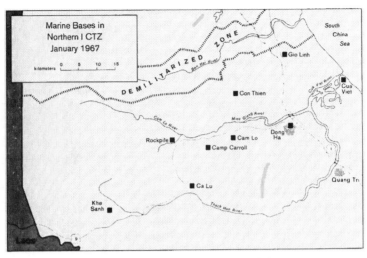

Traveling west from the coast toward the Rockpile the terrain becomes more mountainous. The roadway, #9, is dirt and gravel, and the relative remoteness of Khe Sanh and the *surrounding* hills can be visualized.

ground, varying from small farm plots to dense foliage and triple-canopy jungle — all terrain providing concealment that favors an attacker. It was an understatement that the terrain surrounding KSCB complicated a defense plan for the base. The proximity to the Laos border made things even worse.

American Special Forces mounted intelligence collection activity and intermittent helicopter and scout plane deployments at the airfield, mostly associated with "cloak and dagger" monitoring of NVA activities along the Ho Chi Minh Trail and across the Laotian border. The number of American and allied soldiers doing this work gradually grew through the mid-60s, but the Marine presence was limited. In the spring of 1966, a Marine infantry battalion conducted a search and destroy operation from north to south through the Khe Sanh Valley but met no opposition and left immediately.

In 1966, several attempts were made to dissuade General Westmoreland regarding defending Khe Sanh. At the April 1966 commanders' conference, he asked that all subordinate commands "work up detailed scenarios of what the enemy might do." The MACV commander suggested that the U.S. planners assume that the Communists "will try to suck us into a fight on a field of their choosing." He asked each subordinate

Khe Sanh

Major General Lowell English

commander to war game in order to avoid barging into battle at a disadvantage.

In September 1966, the Marines briefed General Westmoreland with the results of their analytical war game. The Marines recommended to pull back to a line stretching between Dong Ha, Cam Lo, and the Rock Pile, but not hold anything west of the Rock Pile, nor anything north of Route 9. General Westmoreland asked, "I notice you haven't made any comment about putting a force in Khe Sanh. What's your reason for this?" The Marines responded that Khe Sanh would be too isolated — too hard to support. The Marine command resisted Westmoreland's suggestion to put a force in Khe Sanh. Most Marine generals believed that Khe Sanh had no basic military value. Brigadier General Lowell English, the 3d Marine Division Assistant Division Commander, summarized their view as follows: "When you're at Khe Sanh, you're not really anywhere. It's far away from everything. You could lose it and you really haven't lost a damn thing." Despite Marine protests, it became obvious that III MAF would have to defend Khe Sanh.

The catalyst for the decision was a 26 September 1966 intelligence report that pinpointed a North Vietnamese troop concentration and base camp only 14 kilometers northeast of Khe Sanh. Marine Lieutenant General Lewis Walt, Commanding General of III MAF, bowed to the inevitable and ordered the 1st Battalion, 3d Marines (1/3), already on the alert to move to Dong Ha from Da Nang, to move to Khe Sanh instead. This was done reluctantly; the III MAF G-3, Colonel (soon Brigadier General) Chaisson, declared: "We were not interested in putting a battalion at Khe Sanh ... [but] had we not done it, we would have been directed to put it out there . . . we put it out just to retain that little prestige of doing it on your own volition rather than doing it with a shoe in your tail." 1/3 received 12 hours' notice that their next location was to be in Khe Sanh. The 1967 "hill fights" on 881S and 881N that would follow were among the first truly "conventional" battles where Marine units were able to fix the enemy and bring superior firepower to bear against NVA units.

Fought for and won at great cost in April and May 1967, these victories were the Marines' first encounter with significant NVA forces in the Khe Sanh area. Apparently, the NVA were bothered by American and South Vietnam forces using the area as a base for intelligence collection and harassment of NVA logistical and command and control facilities in nearby Laos. They planned to attack KSCB, and the Marines spoiled the plan. However, no sooner were these hills seized than they were abandoned, as the strategy then was to seek contact with the enemy. The hills had no intrinsic value.

Following the Hill Fights and the permanent deployment of 1/3, extensive improvements were made to improve the KSCB airfield. As 1967 came to a close, there were signs of renewed activity: the 325C and 304th NVA divisions were moving into the Khe Sanh region. The year 1967 ended as it had begun: a major invasion of Northern Quang Tri province appeared to be the enemy's next move.

The Siege at Khe Sanh, January 1968

In early January, MACV headquarters was expecting an attack on Khe Sanh — the popular opinion was that it would not happen until after the Vietnamese Tet holiday, 30 January 1968.

Khe Sanh

So, digging deeper and improving defensive fortifications was high on the priority list, and that was fortunate because the first set of attacks was to be sooner than expected, a few days before Tet.

Following a series of CIA and other intelligence reports, there was a rippling of meetings and control actions up and down the chain of command. On 17 January, to strengthen the KSCB defense, a third infantry battalion (2/26) was deployed to Khe Sanh, giving the commander of the 26th Regiment, Col. Lownds, all the men of the 26th Marines for the first time. The new battalion moved rapidly to occupy and begin fortifying hill 558, effectively blocking the avenue of approach to KSCB from the Northwest.

On 18 January, U.S. Navy helicopters from the 7th Fleet began dropping a total of 316 sensors in nine arrays along avenues of approach around KSCB. This was the first test of the technology system of the barrier that would be code-named Operation *Muscle Shoals*. Sensor activations from this untested system would be transmitted to orbiting EC-121 aircraft which amplified the signals and retransmitted them to an Infiltration Surveillance Center at Nakhon Phanom, Thailand (NKP). There, Air Force technicians processed the data with an IBM 360 computer and then transmitted the information to MACV for eventual retransmission to the warfighters at Khe Sanh. Within a week the system was operational.

Although it may have sounded like science fiction at the time, the use of the sensors had great promise. The Marines needed the sensor information because the vegetation in the area made it practically impossible to know who was moving where; and if they knew where the enemy was headed, they could be ready for them or fire on them. The sensors worked but making use of this radically new program required solutions to three problems: (1) unacceptable delays between sensor activation and the receipt of the combat intelligence by the ground commander or his staff, (2) the locations of the sensors, and (3) even if the first two problems were overcome, there was still the problem of how to interpret the information and how best to exploit it.

The ground commanders initially had no say in exactly where the sensors were placed, but the planned sensor locations were generally good, and the sensors worked. The location deficiency was not the planned locations, but the fact that the sensors were not always exactly where they were thought to be. The

Courageous Dissent

Target Intelligence group was seeing sensor activations in very strange places that sometimes confused the true location of the enemy, but over time, they were able to determine which sensor activations to ignore.

The Marines needed timely information. At first, they thought they could use the sensor activation locations for fire missions, but they soon realized that the original concept was just nonviable. The sensor network was reporting movement, but the enemy had moved by the time a fire mission was ready to respond to an activation. And the information from Nakhon Phenom was usually 12 hours old when Khe Sanh received it from MACV in Saigon. The Marines at KSCB could intercept the signals from the EC-121 aircraft, but it was unreadable — just pages of numbers that made no sense.

Fortunately, the Marines did not give up. By studying the signals reports, using known enemy movement locations, and knowing the intended locations activated sensors, Captain Baig was able to effectively decode the activation reports, much like the computers at Nakhon Phenom. Once the Target Intelligence team could do that in a reasonable time, they learned how to interpret the data in terms of size and composition, speed of movement, and likely destination and timing. The battlefield sensor data, when understood and combined with Captain Baig's detailed knowledge of NVA military doctrine, became actionable intelligence that could inform Colonel Lownds of enemy tactical plans. Although the absolute impact of the sensor program on the outcomes at Khe Sanh cannot be fully known, the Marines at Khe Sanh believed it was a game-changer. Certainly, the use of sensors was a portent of other advances in military tactics that would be realized in the coming years. The electronic battlefield was born.

By 19 January, the 26th Marines regimental headquarters, and most of the artillery were at KSCB; 2/26 (-) was at Hill 558, Kilo Company, 3/26 was holding Hill 861, Echo Company 2/26 held 861A (very close to 861), and India Company of 3/26, reinforced with two platoons of Mike Company and three 105 howitzers from the 13th Marines, was securing Hill 881S.

Ten days before the Tet holiday was to arrive, the long-anticipated battle had begun. At dawn on 19 January, India Company sent a reinforced platoon north to Hill 881N to recover a radio and some code sheets. The radio had been left behind on the previous afternoon when a recon team from the Third Re-

Khe Sanh

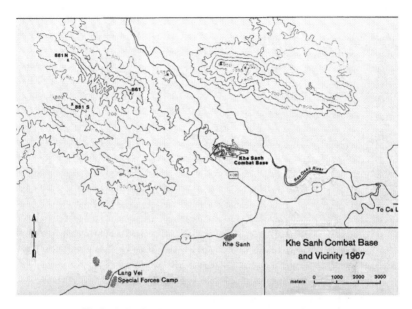

Khe Sanh Combat Base and the surrounding terrain and roads.

connaissance Battalion was evacuated from a tense firefight with an NVA ambush, resulting in two Marines killed and the remaining five Marines wounded. When the platoon approached 881N, it too was taken under heavy fire and was forced to pull back without recovering the lost items.

Realizing that he had a substantial enemy force only two kilometers away, the commanding officer of India Company, Captain William H. Dabney, set out with his entire company in the early morning of 20 January, determined to destroy it. About halfway to the objective, accurate enemy machine gun fire began picking off his lead elements, forcing the company to call for artillery support and a medevac. When the medevac helicopter arrived and approached the landing zone, it was hit by antiaircraft fire and shot down. Captain Dabney's Marines had made some progress, but things had quickly gone from bad to worse. Nevertheless, he was determined to turn things around. So India requested close air support to reduce the objective before continuing the attack, only to be stopped in place and ordered by Col. Lownds to break off the attack and return to 881S. Col Lownds order came at a difficult moment, just as Dabney's Marines had located the enemy and established a plan to take the hill. India

Courageous Dissent

Company had lost four men killed and almost ten times that wounded, and they were not happy about turning tail and giving up what progress they had made.

Captain Dabney was not aware that earlier that afternoon, a North Vietnamese lieutenant, had approached the Northeast side of the KSCB perimeter with a white flag and surrendered. He identified himself as Lieutenant Tonc, the commanding officer of an NVA antiaircraft company in the 325C Division, which was consistent with the current intelligence estimates. Lt. Tonc told the Marine interrogation team that a reinforced battalion was to attack Hill 881S and Hill 861 that very night. He also said that a successful attack of Hill 861 would be followed up by a regiment attacking the base itself. If that were not enough, Tonc said that artillery would be used to support the attack, that tanks might also be used, and that General Giap was directly controlling the NVA campaign that included the Khe Sanh operations.

Col. Lownds reported all these statements immediately to Division Headquarters and to the Special Forces at Lang Vei. Although he did not know what parts of Tonc's revelations to believe, Lownds accepted at face value that there would be an attack that very night, and he elected to limit the number of major battles he would have to support that night by pulling India Company back. The prospect of enemy artillery was not a surprise, as it had been used elsewhere along the DMZ by the NVA, and Lownds was already taking all the precautions that he could to protect his force from artillery. Of course, Lownds knew who General Giap was, and to think that Giap might be directing the enemy campaign was something for his superiors to think about. But the idea of a tank attack may have been outside the bounds of known NVA capabilities that Lownds' intelligence people were ready to accept. The information that Tonc provided flew up the chain of command and was soon in the hands of Saigon and Washington, as well as other American forces in the area.

Should the Americans believe Tonc, or was this a ruse designed to somehow fool them? A gift horse like this was almost too much to accept. But there was nothing to lose by accepting the most immediate threat and preparing for attack on 881S and 861 that night. So, while he acted on many of Tonc's assertions, Lownds did not accept everything.

Lt. Tonc was correct about the attack on Hill 861. That night, just as Tonc had said, bombardment of Hill 861 with rockets, mortars, rifle propelled grenades (RPGs), and heavy machine guns began, and at approximately 0100, an NVA infantry attack slammed into the West side of the perimeter with Bangalore torpedoes, satchel charges, and assault troops. Most of the Kilo Company command structure was killed or seriously wounded, and the perimeter was breached almost immediately, but the Marines gave way only as they were forced to, and Kilo Company maintained its cohesiveness, now under the command of a green 2nd lieutenant. At 0500 the morning of 21 January remaining Marines were able to mount a savage and bloody counterattack, and soon retook their hilltop.

Lt. Tonc was not correct about the attack on Hill 881S. It did not materialize, and it allowed India Company, after some hesitation, to fire 680 rounds of 81 mm mortar shells in support of Hill 861, preventing NVA reinforcement of their attack. This mortar fire was in large part critical to the success of the counterattack. Neither the artillery at the Khe Sanh base nor the 175 mm battery at Camp Carroll could fire effectively on the enemy because the NVA chose to attack on the west side of the perimeter, which was in defilade for fires coming from the east at Camp Carroll. Only mortars were effective in that case, and they were well within range of 881S.

About the same time as the battle for Hill 861 reached a crescendo, a heavy rocket and mortar bombardment of KSCB began. It was not much different from most such "incoming" except that after about 15 minutes, rounds hit the ammunition and fuel dumps and started a fire. The result was the destruction of a huge amount of the ammunition supplies that had been stored there. And until the airstrip could be repaired, ammunition supplies were effectively cut in half. Ammunition of all types and sizes, including heavy mortars and artillery, as well as pyrotechnics, explosives, tear gas, and grenades were cooked off or blown out of the ammo dump and into other positions within the base, and they exploded sometimes in the Marines' defensive position—causing sheer chaos and destruction.

Despite the heavy bombardment, outbound Marine artillery and mortar fire remained active, and surprisingly, there was no NVA attack on KSCB to take advantage of the situation. Warfighters there were able to turn their attention elsewhere. There was no shortage of things for Col. Lownds' staff to attend to. In addition to the very real problems of maintaining an effective defensive posture against possible ground attacks, the

Marines on KSCB were struggling to repair and protect their facilities, most of which were above ground. They began replacing damaged equipment and rebuilding supply stocks, especially ammunition. Between the firing in support of the fight on Hill 861 and the losses at the ammo dump, ammunition supplies had fallen critically low for a command expecting attack.

But on the morning of 21 January, there was another attack going on just three and a half kilometers outside KSCB, at the village of Khe Sanh. There, in the seat of the Vietnamese Huong Hoa District Government, about five kilometers south of KSCB, the Marines of Combined Action Company (CAC) Oscar, the District advisory team, and Vietnamese Regional Force (RF) troops, about 175 men, were fighting for their lives against an NVA regiment of the 304th Division.

This attack, like most others, had been forewarned, so their defenses were ready, and the South Vietnamese government officials at the district headquarters had been able to move to KSCB the previous day. The heavy NVA infantry force attacked just after 5:30 a.m., and the village itself was lost almost immediately, but the CAC Marines defending the District Headquarters were holding on.

The Marine CAC Company Commander, Lt. Thomas Stamper, had previously prearranged fire missions from the artillery at Khe Sanh using variable-timed fusing so that the shells would burst about 20 meters above the ground, increasing the lethality to infantry forces. Stamper called for these fires almost immediately when the attack began, and despite the burning ammo dump at KSCB, the artillery battery was able to shift their guns to this entirely different azimuth and support the defense of the District Headquarters. The Marines and their Regional Forces (RFs) in bunkers with overhead cover were protected from air bursts, but these fires had a devastating effect on the attacking forces.

The hazy dawn of 22 January revealed scores of NVA dead littering the fields of fire around the district headquarters, with NVA survivors now digging in just outside the barbed wire fortifications and continuing to snipe at defenders. The CAC Marines could hold them off for a while, but they would need reinforcement and resupply to make it through the next night.

As close as it was to KSCB, reinforcement was thought by the men at Khe Sanh village to be a quick thing, but the rifle company Col. Lownds sent to help stopped their advance just short of the town, and then was recalled to KSCB after receiving warning of an ambush. Col. Lownds decided against sending men to fight outside his own perimeter because he saw it as playing into the hands of his adversary, making his forces vulnerable to piecemeal destruction. He announced there would be no further attempt to help. This action shocked and dismayed the beleaguered company, who felt they had been abandoned and written off. When Lownds refused to act, an ARVN relief force from 60 kilometers away was dispatched in U.S. Army Special Forces helicopters, but that force was annihilated trying to reach the village.

As night approached, survival prospects for the CAC Marines and the Vietnamese Regular Forces were now dim. But a surprise appearance of a welcome U.S. Air Force "Spooky" AC-47 gunship with large, battlefield illumination flares and electrically-operated gatling guns, repeatedly discouraged further NVA attack ambition. By daylight of 23 January, the attackers had vanished from the battlefield. The Marines and other defenders of the village were able to walk to the base without further enemy activity later that morning.

Later during the day of 22 January 1st Bn, 9th Marines (1/9) arrived at KSCB, having been dispatched there that morning. This increased the number of Marine infantry battalions to four under the command of Col. Lownds in defense of Khe Sanh. They rapidly made their way to a small hilltop near the rock quarry about a mile west of the Base, effectively blocking a possible avenue of approach.

On the morning of 23 January, the fog was just lifting from the valley when an Air Force C-123 cargo plane dived and banked sharply to line up for landing on the air strip at Khe Sanh Combat Base. Captain Mirza (Harry) Baig was seated on the floor of the plane's crowded cargo bay, just like the other Marines making their way to this remote outpost in the Northwest corner of South Vietnam. Baig had given up trying to see out the few portholes in the sides of the cargo bay, but he felt sure that the aircraft was getting close, as it suddenly seemed to swerve and dive, then held steady, jerked to the right, then held steady, and then hit the runway with a hard thud that everyone felt in their bones. The engines again roared as the propeller pitch reversed, and the plane braked to a sudden stop.

The loadmaster yelled to the passengers to brace for landing because there had been heavy fighting in the surrounding hills and the nearby village for the last two days, and a heavy bombardment of the combat base and the airfield, itself. By the time the aircraft came to a stop, the ramp was down at the rear of the plane, and passengers were told to get to their feet and "move it" as fast as they could.

The noise of the C-123's turbine engines was still so loud that no one could really hear the loadmaster, but they all got the idea quickly. Baig had been in-country for many months. Arriving from the 3rd Marine Division headquarters in Dong Ha, he also knew the seriousness of the situation. He also had a general idea that they had only a few seconds before mortar and artillery rounds would start impacting the runway, trying to score big by destroying the plane. So, Baig, wearing an odd Boy Scout backpack, grabbed his "willy peter" bag (a waterproof laundry bag) holding the rest of his possessions, and ran down the ramp and off to the side of the runway with all deliberate haste.

Along with the rest of the passengers, Baig followed the arm-waving of the Marine with the red patches sewn on the sides of his pant-legs, who had come out onto the runway. The red patches identifying him as a landing support specialist. What Baig saw around him as he double-timed to the side of the runway, and as the C-123 again began taxiing, confirmed all that he had heard. The combat base was a combination of broken down hard-backed tents, field expedient bunkers, shrapnel-sprayed equipment, and other detritus of war — oddly reminiscent of a trailer park that had just been hit by a tornado. And the Marines he saw were all wearing helmets and flak jackets. They were dirty from the ubiquitous red clay and their eyes were big and perpetually watchful.

Unlike most of his fellow passengers, Baig knew in detail what had been going on at Khe Sanh, especially in the last six weeks or so. For the last year, the combat base had seen a lot of changes and a lot of nearby fighting. Up until then, there had not been much Marine Corps interest in this valley clearing near the western end of Route 9, in the far northwest corner of South Vietnam. However, its proximity to the Ho Chi Minh Trail, along which most of North Vietnam's support for its "war of liberation" traveled, had made it strategically important to General Westmoreland. The General saw Khe Sanh as the western end of the new barrier along the DMZ and a possible support facility for operations to the west, across the Laotian border. He also saw it as a good place for a confrontation with the North Vietnamese Army.

Captain Baig had recently joined the 26th Marines staff as the new Target Intelligence Officer (TIO.) His appearance and demeanor had an instant impact on the other members of the Fire Support Coordination Center (FSCC). He was short, bespectacled, and probably the cleanest person at Khe Sanh. At his belt was a short, curved kukri dagger instead of the standard Marine Kabar. He spoke with a British accent and phrasing and had an extraordinary vocabulary and analytical mind. Although he came up from the enlisted ranks, he had a steely sense of purpose and destiny, and he had impeccable credentials as both a clandestine intelligence coordinator and as an artillery battery commander. And he was on speaking terms with the Commanding General.

Captain Mirza Baig and Major Bob Coolidge shared the duties of the target intelligence desk in the Fire Support Coordination Center (FSCC) 24 hours a day: Coolidge in the daytime and Baig at night. Baig and Coolidge, along with Baig's assistant, Staff Sergeant Bolsey, set to work immediately assembling, cataloguing and analyzing every piece of real estate within range of available fire support assets. Using the best technology available at the time, they penciled in everything that was known about every 1,000-meter grid square in their own manual geographical information system: a box of 3" by 5" note cards, organized by the map coordinates of those grid squares. They then extracted the data on those cards onto lists that offered quick access to locations that possessed militarily important characteristics, such as reported gun emplacements, radio signals intercepts, possible assembly areas, possible attack, or mortar positions, and observation sites. This information had been reported over a period of many months, and although the data was entered into logbooks, until now most of it was essentially unavailable for targeting in a systematic way. So, even if simple in concept, this painstaking, tedious development work improved targeting in the area by an order of magnitude.

One of the elements of military information Baig and Bolsey catalogued was the electronic sensor insertions around Khe Sanh. The original intention was to use the sensors along the Ho Chi Minh trail, but that would have to wait. Right now, the Marines at Khe Sanh had plenty of other worries. Although they had a sizable and capable force assembled to defend the combat base, they had lost or expended much of the ammunition they needed to assure successful defense of the base. Fortunately, the NVA commanders around Khe Sanh did not exploit the advantages they had achieved with the seizure of the District Headquarters and the destruction of the ammo dump.

The 21 January fighting resulted in 57 Marines killed and wounded, and destroying a helicopter, weather monitoring equipment, the airstrip's night lighting system, bunkers, engineer equipment, generators, a mess hall, and other facilities. Of the material losses, the ammunition dump was most critical; the Marines were not strangers to this threat to their survival in Khe Sanh. The Chu Lai, Dong Ha, and Cua Viet ammunition dumps had already been favorite targets of NVA artillery, destroying tons of bombs, munitions, and aircraft fuel bladders at those sites.

At Khe Sanh, in an attempt to disperse the ammunition, three storage areas had been established. The main dump, hit by a 122 mm rocket, was located on the east end of the combat base, just off the runway and dug in with revetments. Following the attack, III MAF immediately moved to replenish the ammunition lost, but the task was complicated by damage to the airstrip. With only 1,800 feet of the 3,900-foot runway open, large-capacity cargo aircraft could not land. Nonetheless, six light cargo aircraft landed at Khe Sanh after dark on 21 January, bringing in 26 tons of much needed ammunition. After midnight, a helicopter delivered whole blood after an extremely dangerous landing on the "socked-in" airstrip.

Replacing the supplies and ammunition required doubling the tonnage delivered to the base from an average of 126 to 235 tons per day. Resupply to Khe Sanh was by air alone, complicated by the continuing shelling of the base and the hill outposts and the lethal antiaircraft fire trying to bring down those planes. There was too much damage to the C-130 and C-123 cargo flights and to the Marine helicopters to provide resupply flights to the hill outposts, forcing the Marines to resupply them by helicopter directly from Quang Tri or Dong Ha rather than to manage distribution locally. Surprisingly, the NVA allowed air resupply, without any immediate ground attacks at KSCB. To the Marines, it seemed that the NVA was not responding to conditions on the ground.

This was also a time of change for the management of offensive air power in support of Khe Sanh. General Westmoreland saw air power as one of his greatest assets, particularly the B-52 flights out of Guam, the Philippines, and Okinawa. He had directed that the air war prioritize support to KSCB with Operation *Niagara*, which was to start on January 30. Now he assumed part of that control on 22 January by directing that he personally controls the use of all B-52 air interdiction strikes through a new MACV headquarters he established. Although this subverted the process then in place for *Arc Light* management, Westmoreland believed that the Khe Sanh area was strategically important, that it was crucial to hold the Khe Sanh combat base, and that he wanted to personally control his most powerful single asset. The Marines retained great influence in Westmoreland's targeting choices within this directive, including the option to re-task the B-52 flights for good cause up until three hours from target time, so they must have welcomed it.

General Westmoreland also sensed that the Vietnamese should have some stake in Khe Sanh defense, and on 27 January he directed the 37th ARVN Ranger Battalion to report to the 26th Marines. Col. Lownds was now in command of five battalions. Lownds had not requested additional troops and was apparently reluctant to disrupt the defensive alignments and fortifications his men had managed to establish. He was also uncomfortable having Vietnamese moving freely within his perimeter. The employment of this elite battalion was to extend the runway somewhat to the Southeast and add the Ranger Battalion like a blister outside the current lines, with the lines of 1/26 to their rear. However, as time went by this unit proved to be entirely satisfactory and helped beef up the perimeter.

Westmoreland had designated 30 January, the all-important Tet holiday, to send 36 B-52 bombers, carrying 1,000 tons of bombs against a target identified by signal intelligence (SIGINT) inside the Laotian border to be the NVA headquarters controlling forces around Khe Sanh. And in case there was anything left, again after dark, there were nine more B-52s. Following the strike, the radio signals stopped, but the NVA forces elsewhere were, at that point, already in position to initiate attacks on cities and airfields, not to mention innumerable bridges in and around population centers all over the country. This force needed no further guidance from General Giap, who we now know was in Hanoi at the time.

Because of Tet, 31 January was chaos over most of South Vietnam, but at Khe Sanh it did not seem much different from the day before. Some of the units that intelligence said were then in attack positions at Khe Sanh were located three weeks later at blocking positions in the vicinity of Hue City, the old provincial capital, which was hit particularly hard in the Tet offensive. At the 26th Marines' Fire Support Coordination Center, (FSCC), the target intelligence work that had begun in earnest at Khe Sanh a week earlier was continuing unabated.

The Siege at Khe Sanh, February 1968

Things remained quiet at the base until the night of 3 February. An NVA soldier who surrendered at the perimeter back on 22 January told his interrogators he had been told that if the initial attacks at Khe Sanh were unsuccessful, the NVA forces would pull back into Laos until after Tet. They would then return on 3 February with double the force size, more artillery, and tanks. It is not known what credence the Marines gave this report, but that night the *Muscle Shoals* sensors began to announce the presence of a significant force in two areas, one north of 881S and the other north of 861, which had no sensors in its immediate vicinity. Captain Baig initially interpreted this activation data as supply operations, informed the Regimental staff, and initiated artillery missions on the activations with no known results.

On the next night, 4 February, activations resumed and Captain Baig, who had continued to think about the activation patterns of the previous night, studied the new data. Now he assessed the data as reflecting the presence of NVA in regiment strength: 1,500 to 2,000 men, preparing to attack 881S or 861. This time he interpreted the activations not as targets, but as portents of things to come. As activations proceeded, the pattern he saw indicated that they were closing in on 881S, and he recommended that Col Lownds order defensive artillery in the most likely assembly areas and attack positions. These fire missions were completely successful in smashing NVA units there and thwarting this attack — a resounding successful use of the new technology.

Unfortunately, there was also an NVA attack on Hill 861A, a ridge adjacent to 861 that had only recently been occupied by the Marines of Echo Company, 2/26. Because there were no sensors on the approaches to 861, this attack by one or two battalions, initiated by a massive volley of 82 mm mortar rounds, was not forewarned by the sensor system and was a very unwelcome surprise. Echo Company suffered seven dead and 35 wounded, about 25% of the company. After the first shock of the attack, the FSCC at KSCB directed the massed fires of artillery from KSCB, Hill 881S, and Camp Carroll, firing in barrages that completely boxed in 861A, and cut off the NVA assault elements from the reserves it depended on to consolidate their initial successes. The fires of Army 175 mm guns and Marine 105 mm howitzers trapped the attackers and supported a predawn counterattack by the remaining Echo 2/26 Marines

After this action, with time to digest what happened and what the sensors were saying, Captain Baig immediately accepted blame for the NVA successes at 861A. Despite the universal lack of experience with the *Muscle Shoals* sensor system and the spotty deployment of its sensors, which completely missed 861 and 861A, Baig felt that he should have continued to keep in mind that the sensor activations of the previous night indicated two groups of enemy soldiers, but the successful disruption of the attack on 881S dealt with only one of them. Others in the command bunker saw things differently; they saw his success that night as remarkable and the failure to predict the attack on 861 as merely human.

Lang Vei

The spring 1967 NVA attacks at Lang Vei, approximately 4 miles west of Khe Sanh and about five miles east of Lao Bao on the Vietnamese/Laotian border, had demonstrated the NVA penchant for biting off pieces that they could most easily chew, and revealed problems KSCB artillery had in providing fire support for Lang Vei's defense. Now Lang Vei's defenses had been rebuilt and vastly upgraded by the Seabees. The camp housed about 25 American Green Berets and 12 ARVN special forces soldiers managing the operations of approximately 300 Montagnard Civilian Irregular Defense Group (CIDG) troops. Despite Washington's concerns about the security of the airfield at KSCB, the occupants of Lang Vei had complete confidence in the security of their new camp, relying on their sturdy fortifications, their ample stocks of individual and crew-served weapons, and the loyal tribesmen. They viewed themselves as special, which they were, and they preferred to operate away from the conventional military oversight and regulation of the Marine command at KSCB. They were very protective of their autonomy, and in return, the 26th Marines largely left them alone, aside from limited coordination and intelligence sharing.

However, what happened at Lang Vei on the night of February 6th and morning of February 7th showed a very different picture. The 24th Regiment of the NVA 304th Division, bolstered with 12 PT-76 tanks, attacked the Lang Vei camp, and in an intense battle they penetrated the camp's defenses and eliminated resistance within a few hours. The well-armed garrison of over 300 men fought hard but was wiped out. Most of the Americans escaped and survived, but the ARVNs and most of the others were killed or surrendered, never to be heard from again.

When the magnitude of their plight had become apparent, in the very early morning hours of 7 February, Lang Vei radioed for assistance from the Marines at KSCB. After overcoming initial doubts about the presence of enemy armor, the Marine artillery swung into action, firing some 567 rounds of supporting fire, including 68 top-secret "firecracker" rounds that split into hundreds of antipersonnel submunitions just above the ground. The Special Forces also requested that the 26th Marines execute a previously arranged contingency plan to come to their aid. Colonel Lownds declined that request, citing heavy shelling at KSCB and an imminent infantry attack threat there. At about 0320 radio contact with Lang Vei was lost. Air support at Lang Vei had been ineffective, due to poor radio contact with the beleaguered defenders on the ground, coordination problems with the artillery support, and difficulty in picking out targets and avoiding friendlies due to poor visibility from the air. The total artillery support delivered in support of the failed Lang Vei defense was 2,476 rounds, Air Force airstrikes, and at least 67 Marine air sorties. So, it would be unfair to say that KSCB simply turned its back on Lang Vei.

When Colonel Lownds took command of the 26th Marines in August of 1967, he had directed his staff to update their contingency plan for relieving Lang Vei, should it become necessary. And, they must have taken that potential mission seriously because in November they directed a company from 1/26 to exercise their part of the plan to determine how long it would take for them to get to Lang Vei. Avoiding roads and moving tactically, it took that company nineteen hours.

Three months later, when defense of Khe Sanh was becoming much more a matter of concern, III MAF was asked to review this and other contingency plans, and the 3rd Marine Division staff, in coordination with the 26th Marines reviewed and revalidated it. But when the attack came and when the Lownds learned what was happening, he correctly deduced that sending a reaction force to relieve them was not within his current capabilities, and he informed Major General Tomkins, the Commanding General of the 3rd Division, accordingly.

The contingency plan for the relief of Lang Vei, like all such plans, was based on assumptions. Among those assumptions, whether explicit or implicit, were several that were no longer true:

- The camp at Lang Vei would be able to hold out for the 20 hours it would take for a company to arrive.
- Two companies of Marines would be sufficient to turn the tide at Lang Vei.
- Two companies of Marines would be available. (In fact only one seriously understrength company was available that night because reserves had been used to replace many of the recent heavy casualties at Hill 861A.)
- There would not be coordinated attacks on both KSCB and Lang Vei at the same time.
- The relief force would be able to move tactically, but not have to fight its way to Lang Vei through terrain teeming with NVA.
- The NVA would not bring armored vehicles into the fight at Lang Vei. (The "tanks" used for the first time in Vietnam at Lang Vei were really armored personnel carriers, but they carried heavy machine guns and were impervious to small arms fire.)

After Lang Vei

Now the shock waves were reverberating up and down the chain of command, but the 26th Marines had little time to focus on the Lang Vei loss. At 0415 the next day, a reinforced platoon outpost from 1/9, which was defending in the vicinity of a rock quarry two kilometers west of the airstrip, was attacked by a battalion from the NVA 325C Division following a heavy mortar barrage there and at KSCB. The 65-man garrison was reduced to 22 fighting men, but they rallied and held the NVA within the perimeter to a stalemate as ammunition supplies dwindled. A relief platoon from the 1/9 position set out at 0740 and joined up with the remaining defenders, forcing the remaining NVA soldiers to withdraw under wilting fire from the rest of the battalion and artillery fires at KSCB. The light of day revealed some 150 fallen NVA troops and one prisoner. The NVA unit had suffered a catastrophic loss and had nothing to show for it.

For the next two weeks, the Marines found themselves settling into the gloomy and bloody routine for which Khe Sanh is known: weather that precluded most air support, wet living conditions with mud everywhere, heavy daily shelling, and lots of anti-aircraft fire. The transport aircraft arriving at KSCB and the helicopters servicing the hill outposts were the only means of delivering cargo, retrieving the dead and wounded, and bringing in replacements.

On 10 February, a Marine C-130 delivering fuel in bladders was destroyed by NVA fire. Two days later, the Air Force decided that their C-130s were sustaining too much damage and limited its KSCB supply support to C-123s for personnel and parachute delivery for supplies. C-123s could approach more steeply and could take off without first taxiing to the end of the runway, making them less vulnerable to the enemy's attempts to destroy the planes on the ground. Marine C-130s followed suit a week later, and at that point — and for the next several weeks — the base was down to parachute delivery only for most rations and ammunition, dropping in an area between the combat base and the low hills 1/9 was defending. This technique was reminiscent of the French at Dien Bien Phu, but aside from the daily work to retrieve the parachute bundles, it was generally accurate and effective. By 15 March, 852 airdrop missions had been flown for Khe Sanh, and some 90% of the air-dropped supplies were successfully received.

With trying weather and its low visibility challenges, this was a time for testing and proving the feasibility of air support for the U.S. effort at Khe Sanh, and it was a grueling monotony of danger and deprivation. The U. S. Air Force Operation *Arc Light* deployed B-52 Stratofortresses from bases in Guam and Okinawa which made interdiction strikes at enemy concentrations and supply routes. Occasionally *Arc Light* missions would provide close air support to ground combat operations and would commonly deliver a mixed load of 500 and 750 pound bombs, which translates from 27 to over 100 bombs per aircraft depending upon load. Aircraft would fly in three-plane formation cells and release their load from the stratosphere and couldn't be seen or heard from the ground.

Khe Sanh

Because of air support—including interdiction bombing, close air support, and both fixed wing and helicopter borne transport—Khe Sanh maintained its combat power and never was in grave danger. The interdiction bombing was a daily allowance of three 3-aircraft *Arc Light* missions in the Marines' area of responsibility, plus about 25 more *Arc Lights* nearby but outside the Marine area of responsibility. Close air support (CAS) missions averaged about 300 sorties a day despite the poor weather. In addition, a large number of harrowing Marine CH-46D Sea Stallion flights delivered most of the 16 tons per day per outpost for a total of 465 tons in February and an average of 40 tons per day after the weather began to improve. These were costly operations, evidenced by the loss of 33 helicopters destroyed or permanently disabled in resupply operations in support of KSCB from 21 January through 22 March.

As February continued, a sort of stalemate settled in around the combat base. While the defenders of KSCB took care of their logistical needs in the daytime, the NVA were active only at night, other than continual firing of "shoot and scoot" mortar and artillery missions against hilltops and the base. Among the most frequent activities of the NVA was digging trench lines. They used the bad weather to dig and conceal a system of siege trenches, interlaced with supply bunkers, that stretched all the way from Laos to the Khe Sanh area. Despite all Marine bombing efforts to destroy it, the trench system was believed to be drawing closer to the Marine positions on the south and east sides. With the arrival of another NVA artillery battalion, KSCB suffered what would be its heaviest bombardment on 23 February. On this day 1,307 rocket, artillery, and mortar rounds impacted in or near the perimeter. On the next day, shelling included 130 mm shells for the first time, from an area beyond Khe Sanh's own counter battery fires. The Marines were suffering serious casualties, and they worried that these developments were precursors to a heavier enemy attack.

The advancing entrenchments were a matter of serious concern because that tactic, learned by Giap from the French and reminiscent of a famous French military engineer of the seventeenth century, Sebastian Vauban, was used successfully by these same NVA divisions against the French at Dien Bien Phu. The Marines tried every kind of artillery and air strike to destroy the NVA trenches. They concluded that they could not stop the trenching without venturing outside their fortifications, forcing the hand of Colonel Lownds, who regarded any foray outside the wire as playing into the NVA's hands.

The case for doing something was strong, so Lownds allowed an exception. He authorized the commanding officer of 1/26, who had primary responsibility for the perimeter defense, to send a reinforced platoon out on 25 February to determine whether the perimeter fortifications were still intact and to ascertain the presence and location of a troublesome 82 mm mortar position. The patrol was to venture no more than 1,000 meters away from the perimeter, but apparently exceeded that restriction and ventured into a carefully placed ambush.

The result at the end of the day was the virtual destruction of the platoon, with only 10 survivors, all seriously wounded. The rest were killed or taken prisoner. No relief was sent to their aid, as their location was unclear, and the evident combat power and preparation of the enemy troops was such that a large force would have been required. The dead were left in place until after the siege was broken, something normally considered anathema to all Marines. With darkness approaching, the decision was eventually reached to bombard the ambush area with artillery and air strikes. The battalion commander accepted full responsibility for the debacle. He was replaced shortly thereafter, but nonetheless retained the respect of the Marines with which he served.

Ironically, although the patrol was lost, it accomplished much of its mission. It confirmed that the enemy was in position for an attack, that it was using the system of trenches in a sophisticated way, and that it was ready and waiting for Marine units who might venture forth outside of the safety of the combat base. It also supported the Marines' ongoing argument that B-52 strikes should be allowed closer to friendlies than the current limit of three kilometers, taking a potentially decisive weapon away from the battlefield commander where he needed it most. Furthermore, the NVA had learned from experience at Con Thien that they were safe from the B-52 inside that distance, and they used that information to select attack positions at Khe Sanh that were within 3,000 meters.

Fortunately, earlier in February, the Commander in Chief, Pacific (CINCPAC) had agreed to allow B-52 operations outside of 1,000 meters, for emergency circumstances only, and it was tested successfully north of Hill 881S. Now, on the last day of February, on the heels of the lost patrol, and further supported by *Muscle Shoals* sensor readouts, Col Lownds requested emergency diversion of a planned Arc Light to strike the NVA trench system and a series of intelligence targets based on Captain Baig's assessment of desirability as assembly areas for an assault close to the base. The strike was delivered as requested, and it was later determined that it spoiled the attack of an NVA regiment planned for the lines of the ARVN 37th Ranger Battalion.

The NVA nevertheless executed a peremptory attack. Predicted by signals intercepts and sensor alerts, it came earlier than usual at 2130 29 February, and it seemed half-hearted compared to previous efforts. Only one ARVN soldier was wounded, and no one was killed, while the bodies of some 78 NVA soldiers were found in front of the ARVN lines. The only thing better than the warning of the attack was the response of the Marines and ARVN. Two Arc Lights saturated the enemy assembly areas, preventing reinforcement. In addition to the artillery from KSCB and the 175 mm guns at Camp Carroll, the Marines also made effective use that night of the radar controlled Marine A-6 bombers inside the 1,000-meter limit, breaking up the actual attack forces.

Outcomes

With the beginning of March 1968, weather slowly improved. Although death and destruction continued to lurk throughout the 26th Marines' area of responsibility, compared to the series of attacks in February, there was gradual but noticeable lessening in incoming fire and other enemy activity. While forces at Khe Sanh continued the daily tasks of devising ways to get resupply helicopters safely in and out of the hill outposts and keeping the garrison safe from the ever-present threat of incoming fire, General Westmoreland began planning in earnest for Operation *Pegasus*, which would clear out the Route 9 corridor of enemy forces and effect a ground link-up to allow ground traffic in and out of Khe Sanh. The relief of KSCB, Operation *Pegasus*, began on April 1st.

Three months following the end of the siege, Khe Sanh was bulldozed, abandoned, and Vandegrift Combat Base (formerly named LZ Stud located at Ca Lu, a few miles Northeast of Khe Sanh), replaced KSCB as the barrier's western terminus. The *Dye Marker* line was foreshortened, but still existed. But it was destined to be a failure, and its construction and defense would cost hundreds of Marine casualties. A few months later, General Abrams would replace General Westmoreland.

At this writing, 50-odd years after the battle, in the reunited Vietnam there is a small museum on the location of the abandoned Khe Sanh airfield. A few remnants of the conflict there are on display and one can see boasts of a victory of the Vietnamese people over the Marines at Khe Sanh. Although a dwindling number of American men know first-hand that this claim is misleading at best, and although they are not surprised to see it, they know it for what it is: a falsification of the facts. They know that because they lived through it, and they know that Khe Sanh and those key surrounding hills were held until higher authority chose to abandon that unneeded valley and reassign them to a more decisive fight.

Historians still disagree on the advisability of defending the airfield at Khe Sanh, and that debate is much of the reason for this book. This chapter is simply offered as a summary of the battle. Other volumes, many of which are cited in the bibliography, provide excellent narratives of the drama of the battle, which became etched on the minds of Americans from television news.

There is no disagreement that the cost in blood of the Khe Sanh defense was horrific. That cost has been studied extensively by Ray W. Stubbe, a Navy chaplain and veteran of Khe Sanh. Stubbe estimates U.S. KIA at Khe Sanh at near 1000 and enemy NVA KIA at roughly 5,500, measured from the beginning of Operation Scotland to the withdrawal from the Khe Sanh base. Stubbe's estimates are widely quoted and are published by the U.S. Department of Defense on their website (www.dpaa.mil). His estimate differs with Marine KIA 205 and NVA KIA 10,000-15,000 for the 77-day Khe Sanh siege, published by the Marines in 1969.

The differences are significant but are not directly comparable. We estimate 927 friendly KIA's at Khe Sanh, measured from the beginning of the Hill Fights in February 1967 to the closing of Khe Sanh in July 1968: 260 KIA before the siege (198 Hill Fights, 52 Operation Crockett, 10 in Operation Ardmore), 205 KIA during the siege, and 472 KIA after the siege (92 Operation Pegasus, 308 Operation Scotland II and 82 Operation Charlie.) These estimates include attachments and supporting forces, high when measured against the roughly 6,000 men defending there during the siege.

There was tension between the counterinsurgency strategy favored by the Marines, and the conventional war of attrition against enemy main-force units favored by the headquarters in Saigon. This may have resulted in Marine leaders downplaying the size and importance of NVA units near Khe Sanh, while the MACV staff in Saigon were convinced of that threat and may have overplayed the NVA KIA totals. Jack Shulimson, Marine historian, confirms that suspicion in his reporting that different approaches in strategy could have contributed to discrepancies in casualty reports.

The use of "kill ratios" to measure progress in the Vietnam war of attrition worsens the confusion. The Khe Sanh kill ratio ranges from $15,000/200 = 75x$ (perhaps the highest kill ratio in the history of the Vietnam War, indicating a huge victory at Khe Sanh) to $5500/1000 = 5.5x$ (a low kill ratio, indicating a less desirable outcome from the battle of Khe Sanh).

The opportunity costs resulting from the Marine assignment to that defense instead of other operations may be assessed as even more important than KIAs and kill ratios. Could their presence elsewhere have enabled the South Vietnamese to prevent or repel other Tet attacks? And would that have led to a very different impact on public opinion in America? There are no certain answers for these questions.

But did the Marines and ARVN defenders at Khe Sanh fail in their mission? No, Khe Sanh was one of the many fields of battle in Vietnam where these men and others successfully displayed the determination, resilience, inventiveness, and valor that their situation demanded of them. However, the warfighting strategy and decision that determined Khe Sanh was worth defending as an integral part of General Westmoreland's strong point-obstacle system was a mistake, which had been pointed out by Brigadier General English in September 1966. Khe Sanh represents the high tide of a series of poor strategic policies we have examined to this point. Now we turn to a dynamic division commander who would abandon McNamara's barrier line and Westmorland's strong points-obstacle strategy in favor of a warfighting strategy better suited to the Vietnam conflict.

)( )(

Courageous Dissent

Chapter 6

Dewey Canyon
1969

Appear at points which the enemy must hasten to defend; march swiftly to places where you are not expected. —Sun Tzu

The TET offensive was winding down, but intense fighting with the North Vietnamese Army was not. The 3rd Marine Division's tactical area of responsibility (TAOR) was Northern I Corps, the scene of heavy combat between the Marines and North Vietnamese regulars who infiltrated men and supplies into South Vietnam. In "Leatherneck Square" - a quadrangle bounded by Con Thien, Gio Linh, Cam Lo, and Dong Ha- it was commonplace for a single U.S. Marine battalion to operate all alone because of the need for other battalions to man the barrier (aka *Dye marker* or strong point) positions. Morale within the infantry battalions had dropped as casualties and frustrations mounted. The main missions of the 3rd Marine Division were: (1) the destruction of North Vietnamese and local forces in Quang Tri Province and (2) maintaining the barrier positions along the Demilitarized Zone (DMZ) and south to Khe Sanh. There was a big problem: the second mission was making the first mission unachievable.

In the first three months of 1968, the 3rd Marine Division had suffered a high casualty rate: 170 marines killed and 1,200 wounded per month. Division G-2 (Intelligence) estimated that one Marine Division (~ 10,000 men) faced elements of five NVA divisions - the 324th, 325th, 308th, 307th, and 320th, together with several separate battalions (~ 20,000 men). The local NVA headquarters was located north of the DMZ and maintained pressure on the American Marine positions by direct infantry attack and by indirect fire from artillery, rockets, and mortars. Marine bases in the central and eastern DMZ could be hit by the NVA guns located north of the Ben Hai River. Half the Marine casualties were caused by long range artillery weapons estimated to be one hundred 130 mm long range guns, many with twice the range of the Marines' direct support artillery.

When he took command of the 3rd Marine Division, Major General Ray Davis had already served for two months at Provisional Corps Vietnam (PCV), under the command of Army Lieutenant General William B. Rosson. The 3rd Marine Division at Dong Ha was subordinate to PCV at Hue-Phu Bai, the III Marine Amphibious Corps (MAF) at Da Nang, and to Military Assistance Command (MACV) at Saigon. This complex command structure was a source of contention. General Tompkins, Davis' predecessor as 3rd Marine Division commander deeply resented the establishment of PCV. Davis was not concerned. "I did not see having a senior Army command in the Marine zone as a vote of no confidence." Other senior Marine commanders were not convinced.

Fortunately, General Davis already had credibility with his Army boss General Rosson, and he quickly earned the respect of his fellow Army Division Commanders at PCV. He was a close friend with General Rosson; they had been students together at the Army War College. Davis was welcomed as an old friend and treated with respect and courtesy. Inter-service rivalry simply did not exist among the Army Generals and Marine Major General Davis. Mutual respect was a reality.

More importantly, Davis noted how the two Army divisions were organized around the concept of high mobility; helicopters were their primary mode of transportation. The Army was critical of how the Marines used helicopters, and Davis agreed. "We had our operations usually tied to selecting an ideal place for a helicopter to sit down as opposed to sitting down where you can best defeat the enemy. In the mountainous terrain of the western part of Vietnam, the Army started knocking off the tops of hills, emplacing artillery, and 'air assaulting' infantry into these hilltop positions to scour the surrounding area for the North Vietnamese."

"Before-Dark" Dictates

Following the change of command ceremony installing General Davis as the 3rd Marine Division Commanding General, key staff officers and regimental commanders were assembled in the Division conference room. Davis started the meeting by waving a copy of his "yet to be published high-mobility article" slated for the Marine Corps Gazette. He announced, "From this

Dewey Canyon

point on, the Division will use it as a guide." He told them that no longer would the Division guard fixed installations. "I didn't ask or plead with them. I ordered: 'Before dark, these things will happen.' I laid out my scheme... later called my 'before-dark dictates.'"

The next day during the morning intelligence brief, a South Vietnamese Army (ARVN) officer pointed out the location of two major groups of North Vietnamese on the map that covered one wall of the general's plywood office. Davis turned to his aide and told him to order up his helicopter for a flight to the 2nd ARVN regimental headquarters. Twenty-five minutes later, he landed in their command post, completely unannounced.

General Ray Davis while the Commanding General of the 3rd Marine Division.

"I asked Lieutenant Colonel Giai which NVA force the Marines could have," Davis explained. "We agreed that the Marines would attack the northern one immediately. Within minutes, Davis was airborne on the way to the 9th Marines regimental headquarters located a short distance from the Division helipad. After greeting everyone, Davis immediately stepped to the tactical map that covered one wall. He pointed to the suspected enemy location and quickly briefed the commander, Colonel Richard B. Smith, ordering him to coordinate an attack on the enemy force. The quizzical look on the officer's face spoke volumes— "Where the hell am I going to find an extra Marine?"

Davis informed him that two battalions of ARVN soldiers would be placed in operational control of his command within an hour, a Marine battalion was flying in from Khe Sanh, and another was force-marching to join him at that very moment. Within hours four battalions encircled the unsuspecting NVA force and pounded it with massive supporting arms. Unfortunately, many of the NVA escaped because the Marines were slow in completing the encirclement. However, Davis was pleased with the results because the operation introduced the concept of generating overwhelming Marine force by stripping the fixed barrier positions of their infantry. With the success of the first operation, Davis directed that "each of the four or five forward positions where there was a battalion holed up ... or hiding out, as someone coined ... would now have only one company, and the other three rifle companies and the headquarters would deploy as a mobile force to seek out the enemy."

With that decision, Major General Davis, effectively abandoned McNamara's long opposed barrier line by ordering that no unit larger than a rifle company could stay in a fixed position. By the Spring of 1968 it was obvious that the barrier was ineffective. Even with the use of the best available technology it was not possible to totally prevent the advance of enemy forces into South Vietnam. Defending the McNamara line had effectively tied Marine ground units to fixed positions where they became targets for NVA artillery and rockets. Davis knew his Marines were better on the offense than the defense.

This action was in part a result of General Davis having spent those months as the assistant corps commander of the Army's Provisional Corps Vietnam, later named XXIV Corps. He was a first-hand witness to the Army's effective use of helicopter mobility and brought that knowledge to the Third Division. Eight months later, the 9th Marine Regiment would launch Operation *Dewey Canyon*, undoubtedly the Marines' most successful and most effective helicopter assault operation during the entire Vietnam conflict.

Going to air mobility was part of Davis' plan, but not the only part. He also moved to restore unit integrity by bringing each battalion under the control of its parent regiment. Over the preceding three years, battalions had been dispatched to one area or the other to operate under another regiment's command. By the time Davis took command, the division's subordinate units were very much disordered. Battalions were scattered around, many serving outside their usual operating areas and under unfamiliar commanders. Davis ordered all this to end. Thus, when the need arose, the 9th Marine Regiment was whole, with all its subordinate units under its umbrella, including its artillery support, the Second Battalion, Twelfth Marines (2/12). Commanders and staffs came to know each other and attained solid rapport. Marines worked and fought alongside those they knew. This created the necessary unit cohesiveness so essential to successful combat operations and increased the sense of unit pride and esprit in the regiment.

Dewey Canyon

From April 1968 to January 1969, the 9th Marine Regiment, comprised of three infantry battalions and supported by an artillery battalion, spent much of its time fighting the NVA in the jungle-covered mountains of western Quang Tri Province. The high mobility concept was tested there and adjusted multiple times until the regiment was better at mountain warfare than any unit in Vietnam. During the four months from August through November 1968, Echo Battery of 2/12 would occupy 25 different firing locations in direct support of the 2nd Battalion 9th Marines (2/9). Knowing what this regiment could do, General Davis ordered the planning of what would become Operation Dewey Canyon.

Operation Dewey Canyon Background

Early in January 1969, several factors sparked an interest in an area in the far southwestern corner of Quang Tri Province. There, the Laotian border ran north-south along its western side, then zigged east for approximately five kilometers. There, the NVA had reopened Route 922 into the A Shau Valley after many months of disuse. Anti-aircraft units increased activity along the road network both in Laos and the A Shau Valley. American jets received fire; an A-6 aircraft was lost; helicopters and reconnaissance aircraft were being fired at with large caliber automatic weapons.

Traffic on the road in Laos doubled during a short period. At times more than 1,000 trucks a day were sighted. Enemy forces also showed their presence by developing a network of heavily used trails and by using small arms fire against Marine reconnaissance efforts. Sophisticated wire communication nets were sighted. Intelligence reports and other sources indicated the probable movement of enemy forces back into the Da Krong River area, possibly for commitment into the mountains west of Hue and southwest of Quang Tri. From there, the enemy could attack populated areas as far south as Da Nang with speed and surprise, with the anniversary of the 1968 Tet offensive barely a month away. The primary purpose of Operation Dewey Canyon was to deny the enemy access into the critical populated areas of the coastal lowlands. The emphasis was not simply to kill the enemy and capture or destroy his equipment, but to interdict his access routes.

No American force had ever ventured to the southwestern part of Quang Tri Province. In Operation *Dewey Canyon*, the regiment was thrust into the upper reaches of the Da Krong River valley, thirty-five miles west of Hue and forty miles south of its principal support facility at Vandegrift Combat Base. There, the Province bordered Laos and the Ho Chi Minh trail. On the Laotian side of the international border Marines would learn that the NVA had constructed sophisticated roads and an underground headquarters, including storage areas, offices, and a hospital. The area was also a staging area for moving supplies to enemy forces and the Viet Cong operating in the then Republic of Vietnam (RVN).

Advancing from north to south within the planned area of operations (AO) would require an attack across jungle covered terrain as it became increasingly steep. The final objective would be the crest of a range of mountains at the Vietnamese border with Laos. The entire area was mountainous and jungle-covered with complex terrain compartments, forming a large three-sided bowl. A few kilometers south and southeast was the A Shau Valley; where the Da Krong River commenced its flow north, the A Shau opened to the south. Between these two valleys, dominating the area, was a large hill mass, Hill 1228, called Tiger Mountain. At this point Route 922 entered the A Shau from Laos. On the Laos-Vietnam border to the west, Co Ka Lui a 1,100-meter razorback ridge, dominated the western portion of the AO. Thus, when the operational part of Dewey Canyon began, the Marines were in a three-sided compartment facing uphill into a heavily defended NVA fortress.

In January 1969, the northwest monsoon season was in its final month. Although there was no significant rainfall there was continual cloud cover for periods of as long as a week to ten days, during which normal resupply and evacuation procedures by helicopter were impossible. During the operation, therefore, numerous problems arose which spelled potential disaster. The way they were handled, the concepts that were revised and the ones that were developed to meet these challenges form a part of Marine Corps history.

Route 922 runs west to east along and across the international border where it becomes Route 548, which then runs into the A Shau Valley, one of the enemy's main supply routes in I Corps. It was easily visible from the air, although some of its offshoot roads and trails were well camouflaged. Extensive facilities for receiving and distributing supplies and personnel coming into the country were located along this road network. Given all

Dewey Canyon

Route 548 as it heads south into the A Shau Valley dissects this picture from bottom center to the top as it crests a distant ridge. As seen from the top of Tiger Mountain.

that evidence of enemy activity directed at the populated coast, General Davis was anxious to stop the NVA from moving.

As the operation developed, it was divided into three distinct phases. Phase I consisted essentially of getting the regiment into the AO and establishing fire support bases (FSBs) to support the scheme of maneuver. Phase II consisted largely of patrolling around the FSBs to clear out any enemy prior to launching into the hard target area. Later in Phase II, forces were aligned to jump off into the critical Phase III. Phase III was visualized as a three-battalion, regimental offensive conducted conventionally. At this critical point the operation departed from the high mobility concept. Heavy anti-aircraft (AA) defenses in the hard target area convinced the Commanding Officer (CO) of the 9th Marines, Colonel Robert Barrow, not to risk a heavy loss of helicopters and troops with a heliborne assault into the area. He chose instead to make the final move overland, securing the ground and permitting helicopter resupply and support activities to continue from north to south over ground that had already cleared by infantry. As a result, only one helicopter was lost during Phase III.

Phase I

Phase I dealt with establishing the 9th Marines in an area far from any friendly fixed position. On 19 January FSB Henderson, about eight kilometers southeast of the town of Ca Lu, was reopened in conjunction with a brief clearing operation in the Ba Long Valley around Henderson. Farther south on 20 January, FSB Shiloh and FSB Tun Tavern, used by the 9th Marines in earlier operations, were reopened. On the 22nd, Second Battalion, Ninth Marines (2/9) conducted a heliborne assault into the northern part of the *Dewey Canyon* AO. Its purpose was to open FSB Razor approximately eight kilometers south-southeast of Shiloh and in an area near the Da Krong River in the western part of the AO. Except for scattered small arms fire, the initial assault was unopposed, and work on FSB Razor began immediately.

Razor was like the other sixteen FSBs constructed by the 9th Marines during their earlier period of mountain warfare but was more difficult than most. Trees measuring three to four feet in diameter had to be cleared. The slope on one side was gentle but not easily cleared. Bulldozers were brought in by helicopter to clear the area and to build gun pits and ammunition berms. Work started on the 22nd and the 2nd Battalion, 12th Marines moved Fox Battery into FSB Razor on the 23rd. Also, on the 23rd, the 9th Marines command post (CP) moved into Razor, its 13th displacement in eight months of operations in the mountains. A minimum of equipment was taken along, and the move was smoothly executed. Control of the communications was passed from a position in a rear area to Razor all at one time, and without a shut-down. The artillery battalion CP also moved to Razor on the 24th without losing continuity or centralized fire control. On the same day, Third Battalion, Ninth Marines (3/9) conducted a landing approximately eight kilometers south-southeast of Razor to construct FSB Cunningham and to conduct saturation patrolling in the area. This area had been cleared in large measure by aviation ordnance. The move was uneventful. The next day the artillery battalion moved its Delta Battery and Mortar Battery into Cunningham, completing Phase I.

As the operation progressed, Tun Tavern was closed, leaving the Marines under the protection of three FSB's (with two more yet to be created) but far from any allied base. They were alone with the enemy. FSB Cunningham became the center of opera-

Dewey Canyon

FSB Razor

tions. From an artillery standpoint Cunningham was ideally located. It was almost dead center in the critical part of the AO and its eleven-kilometer fan extended south and southwest almost to the limit of the AO. For this reason, and as the battalions launched their attack south, both the Ninth Marines CP and the artillery CP and fire direction center displaced to Cunningham. During the operation as many of five artillery batteries—two 105mm, two 155mm and the 4.2-inch mortars—were firing from Cunningham at one time.

Late in January two battalions from the Army of the Republic of Vietnam (ARVN) 2nd Regiment were lifted into the *Dewey Canyon* AO east of Cunningham. Kilo Company 3/9 had secured a zone for this move and had begun construction of FSB Lightning.

Phase II

Phase II began on January 24th and 25th as the Marines of 2/9 and 3/9 cast out their companies 2000-3000 meters apart across the *Dewey Canyon* AO, all north of the east-west axis of the Da Krong River. Enemy encountered in this area were screening elements for forces farther south in the hard targets along Route 922. They were trained guides, porters, and troops who

"Middle of Nowhere"—Marine UH-1E (Huey) helicopters touch down with their loads at Fire Support Base Cunningham. Artillerymen of the 12th Marines at Cunningham are supporting elements of the 9th Marines conducting search and clear operations in operation Dewey Canyon. (Photo by LCpl. M.C. Patterson). Sea Tiger, Feb 28, 1969, Vol V, No. 9

kept the lines of communication open. On the 25th, a patrol from Mike Company 3/9 found a four-strand telephone line which ran from Laos into Base Area 101 south of Quang Tri. The lines were strung between tree-mounted insulators. Branches were cleared for the wires, but overhead concealment was maintained so the line was invisible from the air. Enemy troops in the area were evidently devoted to keeping this communication line open. Another early significant find was NVA Field Hospital 88 near the Da Krong River. It contained a fine, large assortment of Russian-made stainless steel surgical instruments, medicine, and facilities typical of a permanent hospital. In any case, the enemy in the Phase II area worked in small bands, many of them living off the land.

The twofold purpose of Phase II was to clear the area around the FSBs and to move gradually into position for Phase III. This placed 3/9 on the eastern flank of the regimental attack and 2/9 on the western flank near the Laotian border. First Battalion, 9th Marines (1/9) would be introduced into the middle when Phase III was ready to begin, while the other two battalions started maneuvering their companies into position. Phase Line Red, the line of departure for Phase III, ran along the Da Krong River's east-west axis. Golf Company 2/9 was on the western flank and was ordered to seize the critical Co Ka Leuye ridgeline, which provided clear observation into the AO beyond Cunningham to the east. Fox Company 2/9 was given the task of constructing FSB Erskine so that its battalion would be under an artillery fan as it approached its objective to the south.

Thus far, all had gone well. The areas around the FSBs were cleared of enemy and the Marines were reaching the Phase III Line of Departure. Then the weather intervened. Just as 2/9 and 3/9 were reaching their positions to commence Phase III and the regiment was preparing to place 1/9 in the center, foul weather set in. It was not a typical monsoon rainstorm, but the visibility and ceiling were in most cases close to zero. Recent experience indicated it would last two or three days and would not change the plans. With the rations and water available to the troops, it was decided to continue preparations for Phase III and to be ready to jump off as soon as the weather lifted.

But on February 3, after four days of very bad weather, Colonel Barrow, a highly decorated veteran of the Korean War, had to decide: should present positions be held? Should Golf Company continue its laborious climb up Co Ka Leuye, or would this be a dangerous extension? Barrow believed that the bad weather would continue, so 2/9 and 3/9 were ordered to pull their companies in and hold them close to areas from which they could be supported. It was not an easy decision, but it turned out the be the right one. The FSBs were stocked with rations and limited water was available. 2/12 had attempted to stock extra artillery ammunition, but the weather had hampered their effort.

Rifle companies operated within the eight-kilometer fan of the artillery on the FSBs so that any company was near food and water and in close mutual support of other companies. In the case of 3/9, Lima Company was on Cunningham; India, Mike, and Kilo Companies moved close to Lima and set in. 2/9 had Hotel Company on Razor, Fox Company on Erskine, and Echo Company at LZ Dallas. Golf Company had the greatest problem. As it moved back from the top of Co Ka Leuye on the morning of February 5 it encountered a large enemy force. The ensuing firefight resulted in 5 Marines killed and 17 wounded. At this point, the company was out of rations, low on water and had dead and wounded to carry out. It took Golf four days to move back to a point where, with a slight break in the weather, it could get some resupply and be relieved of its casualties. As the company reached low ground, Marine aircrews made heroic efforts to extract the casualties. In the worst weather, medevac helicopters flew south up the Da Krong River Valley, and after having been fired on from the high ground on both sides, got in and got out.

As the weather was closing in, the AVRN battalions and their artillery were still being inserted around FSB Lightning, but they were not fully into position. Only one tube of the six-gun 105mm battery had been landed with 100 rounds of ammunition. Both ARVN battalions had only the supplies carried by the troops—a maximum three days of rations, for example. The ARVN situation was desperate. A helo-parachute drop solved the problem by directing helicopters over the target with the air support radar team (ASRT) at Vandegrift. This was at extreme range for the ASRT –over thirty miles—but the first drops landed within 300 feet of the ARVN headquarters. Enough supplies were delivered this way to prevent any long-term deprivation.

Additional ASRT-controlled drops were made from KC-130s into the area adjacent to Marine operations. The KC-130s could drop greater quantities of supplies, but they were less accurate than the helicopters. This increased the difficulty in locating and recovering the drops. These experiences led to refinement of the facilities on Cunningham. For the first time in mountain operations an ASRT was installed at a forward fire support base. In addition, a small logistical support area (LSA) was built permitting stockpiling of additional supplies for delivery to the forward companies on day-to-day operations.

Another innovation paying high dividends involved handling casualties in the field when the weather precluded medevac. Back in November 1968, under the guidance of the regimental executive officer, the three battalion surgeons and the regimental surgeon had fabricated aid stations and special equipment that could be put in boxes for helicopter lift and inserted into FSBs/ LZs, making a small aid station/field hospital in a forward area a possibility. One of these was placed on Cunningham soon after the opening of the base, and it paid for itself a hundred-fold.

Dewey Canyon

When NVA artillery and mortars hit Cunningham, almost continuously whenever the weather went bad, the battalion surgeon and his small aid station saved numerous lives.

But all was not easy back at Cunningham. It was the largest of four fire bases established in the northern A Shau Valley to support *Dewey Canyon* and sat atop a 2,100 -foot ridgeline within five miles of the Laotian border. The ridgeline ran linearly east to west with a sharp cliff to the south and a gentler slope to the north. A ceasefire was set to begin for Tet, the Lunar New Year, and at midnight of 16 February the Marine guns fell silent.

At 0350 hours on the morning of 17 February, the silence of the ceasefire was broken by exploding mortar shells falling on the Cunningham positions. This was quickly followed by a spearheading force of NVA sappers, backed by a supporting force of unknown size, attacking Cunningham on its eastern side. The NVA sappers, or demolition experts, clad only in loincloths and rubber sandals and carrying satchel charges and grenades in vests strapped to their bodies hit the middle of the Marine line. The Cunningham perimeter was guarded at the time by 3/9's Lima Company. The company was thinly spread out, so the ensuing battle became one of infantry and artillery together with cooks, mechanics, clerks, radio operators, engineers, and assorted support Marines on the defense.

The sappers were able to penetrate the perimeter wire and rushed toward the Marine artillery positions dropping satchel charges and grenades into bunkers and fighting holes. Near hand-to-hand fighting resulted and some of the enemy were slain within three feet of the Leathernecks' guns. At the same time, the Marines began to receive a heavy volume of fire from outside their defensive perimeter as the NVA infantry attempted to silence a section of outer lines of defense.

The Fire Direction Center (FDC) of the artillery battalion was damaged, and the watch officer knocked unconscious, by several blasts which also scattered radios and FDC Equipment. However, technical fire direction was automatically decentralized in accordance with standard instructions, and the battalion continued its support missions without interruption, while the batteries on Cunningham fought in defense of the position.

Captain Harvey Barnum, a Medal of Honor winner from previous actions, commanded the 105 mm battery Echo 2/12, which suffered direct hits by the enemy that destroyed Echo's gun number one. The Battery employed their remaining guns

Echo 2/12 Gun #1 position destroyed, parapet and ammunition bunkers leveled.

to fire illumination and lowered muzzles to fire successive blasts of "beehive" shrapnel into the invading NVA. Communications and centralized control were quickly reestablished throughout the position. The battle was over by full daylight. Four Marines died, but daylight found thirty-seven dead NVA. With body parts everywhere, and with artillery firing into the rear of the attackers, it was impossible to tell how many casualties the enemy suffered. The next day three companies from the Second Battalion, Third Marines (2/3) took over the defense of Cunningham, freeing Lima to join its battalion in the upcoming fight.

Weather cost the regiment some of its momentum, and the jump-off position had to be regained. More critically, it gave the enemy time to strengthen their defenses to the south, move additional men into hardened emplacements, and to emplace his artillery and mortars. They were therefore better prepared to meet the attack as the Marines moved toward the hard target area in Phase III.

Phase III

The week-long delay had ended on 11 February when the weather cleared sufficiently to launch Phase III. Each battalion in Phase III had a zone of action about three miles wide—a total regimental zone of approximately nine miles east to west. Each had to fight uphill from north to south and fight the enemy over roughly five miles before reaching the regimental objective at the Laotian border and the real fight.

Although the operation had been planned for each battalion to jump off at the same H-hour, loss of momentum in Phase II made this impractical. 3/9 moved out on 11 February; 1/9 and 2/9 launched the next day. The highest point in the target area was Tiger Mountain at 1,228 meters. Route 922 and the regimental objective were on a common ridgeline running from Tiger Mountain to the south, southwest and then due west. As the Marines moved across Phase Line Red, they made immediate contact. Some prepared enemy positions were not occupied, possibly because the enemy had elected to defend in strength elsewhere. Still, the Marines were up against numerous prepared and occupied positions. The opposition in some cases was determined and formidable. Enemy forces stayed in their bunkers and fighting holes until they were overrun and destroyed. For example, during five days in mid-February Kilo Company had 12 significant contacts, most against bunkers. The whole effort on the part of the NVA was to delay the Marines' advance to Route 922. The Marines were subjected to mortar and rocket-propelled grenade rounds daily but particularly at night. The enemy proved to be well-trained, well-equipped, and tenacious. At night, they attacked squads or platoons against companies. Snipers frequently were tied in trees with no future but to die, an example of the enemy's fanaticism.

At this time, 3/9 had only three companies because Lima Company was at FSB Cunningham for security, a problem soon to be remedied. 1/9 jumped off with their four companies. Both attacked down ridgelines with one company following in trace of another. As a company moved up a ridgeline and made contact, deployed to meet the enemy, and overcame it, a following company could construct an LZ, provide mortar support, and take care of casualties. More importantly, while the lead company re-

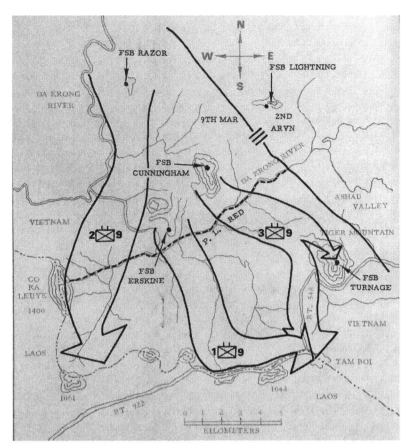

Phase III: Four fire support bases and infantry movements crossing Phase Line Red.

organized, the follow-on company prepared to pass through and resume the attack, thus putting fresh forces into the action and ensuring constant momentum. This worked very well, but a full battalion was required. Therefore, early in Phase III, General Davis ordered the insertion of elements of the Third Marine Regiment to relieve the troops on the FSBs. Two companies of Second Battalion, Third Marine Regiment (2/3) relieved the companies on Cunningham and Erskine. This allowed both 2/9 and 3/9 to operate with all four of their rifle companies.

The first noteworthy find occurred in 1/9's area. The lead element of Charlie Company, after overrunning a bunker complex, discovered two 122mm field guns, extremely accurate weapons with a range of 13 miles. The inspired troops soon

Dewey Canyon

overcame the defenders and captured the guns intact. These two pieces, the largest field guns captured in the Vietnam war, were subsequently evacuated in mint condition. One of these is now on display at the National Museum of the Marine Corps in Quantico, VA.

As the battalions moved south out of range of the supporting guns at Cunningham, it became obvious that a new FSB was needed. As 3/9 approached Tiger Mountain and Route 922, the NVA defense was not heavy, so one company was ordered to take the entire mountain and build FSB Turnage on top; Echo Battery was lifted in to Turnage on 25 February. 3/9 was directed to concentrate its efforts on Route 548 going south toward what turned out to be an enemy stronghold in the Tam Boi area. The advancing Marines made continuous contact on the road, killing many NVA, and subsequently moved into Tam Boi. Here they found a very large, formidable complex with subterranean caves and tunnels, and areas for housing enemy personnel, communications, a headquarters, and large stores of ammunition and food.

In the 2/9 area vehicles were heard moving down the road. On 21 February, Colonel Barrow decided to move across the border into Laos and interdict Route 922 by ambush. On the night of 21-22 February, Hotel Company moved 1,500 meters south in pitch blackness, found and crossed the road, and set up a classical ambush. The ambush was triggered, capturing three vehicles, and the company then swept from south to north picking up miscellaneous gear. One of the captured trucks carried about five tons of ammunition which exploded in a prolonged cook-off.

On 26 February, Delta Company moved east astride Route 922 toward Hill 1044. After eliminating a reinforced NVA platoon occupying the hill, the Marines uncovered the largest arms and ordnance cache of the war. For a week Delta Company continually uncovered caches of enemy supplies in the immediate area. Most of the supplies were buried in the bottoms of scattered bomb craters. The NVA had dug out a hole in the crater, filled it with weapons and ammunition and then recovered it, leaving the bottom of the crater flat and therefore easily recognizable at close range. Almost all the weapons were new, wrapped in oilcloth or canvas and coated with cosmoline. The total haul amounted to over 900 individual crew-served weapons, 80 tons of food stuffs, and 200 tons of ammunition of all sizes. This action virtually nullified the enemy's ability to strike out at civilian and military targets to the east, and any attempt to rebuild this base would be a long and arduous one.

While the Marines were enjoying huge successes over the NVA, they also were experiencing critical and persistent problems. It was impossible to resupply rifle companies without stopping their forward progress and without pinpointing their positions. Often, companies being resupplied received mortar fire. To make matters worse, when a company had received its supplies and was ready to continue its advance, a squad or platoon often had to be left behind to secure the nets, water cans and other items until they could be retrieved by a helicopter. This reduced the company's overall strength and unity and left a smaller unit exposed. Control by the company commander was difficult. An effort was made to improve this situation using disposable packaging, C-rations, ammunition, and water in plastic containers were placed on wood pallets and bundled on discarded or surveyed canvas instead of the usual nets. The bundle was slung on inexpensive loop type wire cables and taken out to the company. The Marines could obtain their supplies, dispose of the packaging, and continue to advance, quickly getting out of the way of incoming mortar fire.

Casualty replacement also became a problem. Some units were sustaining moderately high casualties and began to lose some of their strength and effectiveness. Many needed more men but delivering them was a problem. There was rarely time to stop long enough to cut an LZ capable of taking a troop lift, so Marines were landed with a follow-on company which had been in position long enough to build an LZ. They could then easily join their parent unit as they passed through. Some success was achieved through this method, but it was developed only through its initial stage.

One of the last major fights of the operation occurred on 22 February when Alpha Company, commanded by First Lieutenant Wesley Fox, came upon a heavily entrenched and well-concealed NVA position. Although incoming artillery and mortar rounds spread destruction, and although twice-wounded, Lieutenant Fox rallied his men in a direct attack into the face of the enemy, overrunning the position and leaving the Marines in control of the ground. For his actions above and beyond the call of duty, Fox was awarded the Medal of Honor two years later by President Nixon.

FSB Turnage atop Tiger Mountain

By the end of February, the three battalions had nearly run out of real estate. They had advanced south to the border of Laos, had made a thorough search of the area and were mopping up what enemy supplies they could find. It was time to phase out the operation. A retrograde movement was planned to get the regiment out by reversing the process of the first week. The FSBs would be occupied backward, and the forward ones would be closed one at a time. 2/9, which had been out the longest, would go back first, lifting as a battalion to Vandegrift. 3/9 would follow and 1/9 would remain behind for several more days to finish exploiting the area where Delta Company had made its finds.

But once again, the weather had other ideas and closed in on 1 March. The FSBs had supplies sufficient for as long as two weeks, though not necessarily in comfort. The rifle companies, however, were not so well off. They had been moving constantly and stockpiling was impossible. The troops carried a normal load of five days food and four canteens of water. They had ample ammunition provided there were no heavy contacts. The distance made it impossible to reconsolidate around the FSBs as before. The only recourse was to continue to operate and wait it out.

The helicopters of Marine Air Group 39 and supporting units from the 101st Airborne Division were then to enter their period of greatest trial. Existing logistical support at Quang Tri and Camp Evans were immediately expanded and stocked. These, together with the Logistical teams at Vandegrift, kept helicopters standing by to deliver much needed supplies as soon as the weather permitted. When the clouds cleared in the *Dewey Canyon* AO, for example, it might still be socked in nearer the coast at Vandegrift and Quang Tri, with only Camp Evans, farther inland, able to launch aircraft. Even so, a thick layer of clouds clung to the mountain ranges around the AO and the helicopters could penetrate it only at great risk.

Something new was needed. Only the Marine pilots and aircraft had the full qualifications and instruments to fly in this weather, so helicopters would lift off the LSA and ascend through the clouds on the ground control approach (GCA) bearing until they broke through, usually at around 2,000-3,000 feet. After passing over the mountains they would descend, hoping to find a hole in the clouds. The fire bases and company positions, however, were not always completely open, and the pilots often had to find an opening in the cloud cover before they could get down. The tremendous skill and raw courage of these pilots made this system work. While the weather was marginally operational for no more than three hours at a time, the helicopters were getting in with at least some support.

Inevitably, there were problems. Delivering loads was extremely difficult to coordinate. The distance between the LSAs made communications slow and cumbersome. As requests for resupply were received, the individual LSAs were in some doubt as to who should deliver. It was not simply a matter of assigning a task to a single LSA, for it was impossible to forecast which one would be open when, and logistics personnel were kept busy trying to coordinate resupply.

The weather broke long enough for 2/9 to be extracted on 4 March. 1/9, with its huge cache exploited completely, was directed to move to Tam Boi as a covering force for other friendly units. But from 14 to 18 March, adverse weather prevented extraction. Each day, enemy probes and mortar attacks increased, and on the morning of 18 March, just before dawn, the enemy attacked in company strength supported by mortars. The final

Dewey Canyon

assault was repelled, and by noon the ground fog had cleared enough to commence extraction. Although an extensive suppressive fire plan had been developed to include artillery, fixed wing, and helicopter gunships in addition to organic battalion weaponry, all helicopters, except the final four lifts, were subjected to enemy mortar fire. Miraculously, this total battalion lift under constant enemy indirect fire was accomplished without loss of a single helicopter. 3/9 was lifted out 17 March. On 18 March, 1/9 was extracted, and Echo Battery was lifted out of FB Turnage to Ca Lu, followed by the remaining artillery batteries. Operation *Dewey Canyon* was officially terminated.

Outcomes

In early 1969, NVA engineer units that had been inactive for several months reopened Routes 922 and 548, branches of the Ho Chi Minh Trail that serviced Base Area 611, a logistics depot in Laos and South Vietnam. Base Area 611 enabled the NVA's 6th Regiment, 9th Regiment, 65th Artillery Regiment, and 83d Engineer Regiment to infiltrate into South Vietnam through the Da Krong and A Shau Valleys to Base Area 101, southwest of Quang Tri, and Base Area 114, west of Hue. In the 1968 TET offensive, the NVA had funneled supplies from the Ho Chi Minh Trail into the same two Base areas, following a different route through the Ba Long Valley, a corridor that began around fifteen kilometers east of Khe Sanh. Base Area 611 was a significant problem.

In Operation *Dewey Canyon*, the 9th Marines disrupted enemy operations in the Da Krong and A Shau Valleys and reduced the NVA's ability to supply forces deeper inside the Republic of Vietnam. They seized and destroyed two medium artillery batteries, one light artillery battery, antiaircraft capabilities in the region, and headquarters and storage facilities of an estimated NVA regiment. The Marines destroyed the enemy's regional command control apparatus, eliminated a series of headquarters establishments, and inflicted over 1600 casualties on the North Vietnamese Army. The enemy's engineer and transport capabilities were severely diminished. Additionally, the Marines captured over 1000 tons of weapons, equipment, and supplies; including individual weapons, infantry crew-served weapons, antiaircraft guns, field artillery pieces, vehicles, small-caliber ammunition, and rice.

All three infantry battalions of the 9th Marine Regiment made significant contributions to Dewey Canyon. The destruction of enemy bunkers and weapons caches was astonishing:

1st Battalion: Alpha company discovered a weapons cache, the size equivalent to what a Marine force service regiment would hold. The official tally, most likely an undercount, took two days to complete and included 629 rifles, 60 machine guns, and 19 antiaircraft guns. Charlie company found a 50-ton ammunition dump in a narrow saddle feature of Hill 1044, with easy access to the main supply route. Delta Company uncovered a weapons storage area, the largest arms and ammunition cache of the war to date with more than 100 tons of munitions and hundreds of small arms.

2d Battalion: Fox company discovered the NVA 88th Field Hospital near the Da Krong River when sweeping the area around Fire Support Base Razor and Landing Zone Dallas. An entire complex, the hospital had eight permanent buildings, including an operating room, and enough space for more than 150 patients. It was stocked with Soviet-made stainless- steel surgical instruments and 500 pounds of medical supplies. A well-cultivated, six-acre corn field was found near the hospital.

3d Battalion: Lima and Mike companies found two spiked 122mm field guns, three prime movers, large ammunition, and training areas. The comprehensive tunnel and cave complex surprised the Marines, who found tunnels between 40 – 250 meters long dug into solid rock that could survive direct hits from air and artillery attacks.

The Commanding General of XXIV Corps, U. S. Army Lieutenant General Richard Stilwell released the following statement:

> Dewey Canyon deserves some space in American military history by sole reason of audacity, guts, and magnificent inter-service team play. There was a calculated gamble on weather, and for the most part it was won. If the weather had held throughout, the greater momentum would have made surprise complete, with proportionately greater results. But the troops pressed on through marginal weather, enduring real privation. And somehow minimum essential supply and evacuation went on.
>
> I cannot applaud too highly the airmen of the 1st Marine Aircraft Wing in a variety of dangerous roles, the 101st Airborne Division HOK Company dedicated to the operation, the fighter pilots

(Marine and Air Force) who managed to penetrate the overcast and deliver devastating close air support and effective interdicting blows.

Above all, though, a Marine regiment of extraordinary cohesion, skill in mountain warfare, and plain heart made Dewey Canyon a resounding success. As an independent regimental operation projected 50 kilometers (as the crow flies) from the nearest base and sustained in heavy combat seven weeks, it may be unparalleled. Without question, the 9th Marines' performance represents the very essence of professionalism.

He was so impressed with the Marines' valor that he nominated the 9th Marine Regiment and supporting units for the Army Presidential Unit Citation, awarded the following year. It was well-deserved and was earned by no other unit of Marines in the five years of Marine combat in Vietnam. (*See* Appendix E). It should be remembered that the success of *Dewey Canyon* has its origins in General Davis' "Before Dark" dictates, his advocacy for abandoning the barrier strategy, and his implementation of a high mobility strategy.

)( )(

Courageous Dissent

Chapter 7

Aftermath

May we never confuse honest dissent with disloyal subversion. — *Dwight D. Eisenhower*

Fight for the things that you care about. But do it in a way that will lead others to join you. — *Ruth Bader Ginsburg*

On 17 Feb 1971, George Carver, CIA Special Assistant Vietnam (SAVA) had attended daily meetings in the situation room of the White House for the past week. The Washington Special Action Group (WSAG) top secret meetings were chaired by Henry Kissinger, National Security Adviser to President Nixon. The purpose of the WSAG was management of Operation Lam Son 719, an operation to invade Laos and cut the Ho Chi Minh Trail. Located in the Laos Panhandle, Tchepone was the key objective of *Lam Son 719*.

Enemy contact around Tchepone was described as light at the WSAG meeting on 16 February. The assault on Tchepone was likely to occur in the next 3-5 days, which was good news for the *Lam Son 719* operation. But the Ho Chi Minh trail was only part of the military story in Laos. In many ways, the fighting in Long Tieng, located near the Plain of Jars in the northern region of Laos, was as important as Lam Son 719. The U.S. CIA headquarters in Laos, the Lao Meo tribal headquarters for their commander General Vang Pao, and the country's largest and most important military airfield were all located at Long Tieng.

For years in the Plain of Jars, the struggle between the Laotian government and Communist forces had swung back and forth with the monsoon seasons. Long Tieng was ten miles south of a defensive line known as Skyline Ridge, which ran twenty miles from Ba Na in the north to Pha Dung in the southeast. In 1970, Long Tieng had survived the NVA's offensive, but in 1971, the Communist forces were clearly on the rise, had seized new positions, and were threatening again. In this cyclical war Long Tieng had always been a launching point for offensives in the rainy season in order to re-take territory that had been lost to the NVA the year before. Because the North Vietnamese had been making steady progress in this seasonal see-saw, defending Long Tieng had special significance for the U.S. government. The WSAG, Kissinger, and President Nixon had good reason to be concerned.

It was reported at the 16 Feb meeting that the Long Tieng area was being hard-pressed, and General Vang Pao had been shaken by a heavy rocket and mortar attack on his headquarters. Hundreds of Thai regular army reinforcements had been moved in. B–52 and tactical air support was being provided. Heavy fighting was anticipated over the next 6–8 weeks. On 17 Feb 1971, Carver, sent a telegram—called a cable in those days—to the CIA Chief of Station in Vientiane, Laos. The cable (still Secret today and printed here with redactions) reads as follows:

> Per your interest in breaking Ban Na siege with air power along Khe Sanh model, you should be aware of presence in Bangkok of Major (possibly now Lt.Col.) Munir M. (For Mirza) Baig, USMC, whose mailing address is Box 363 US MACTHAI/JUSMAG. Baig was intelligence and fire control officer at Khe San during 1968 battle who did much to develop and operate close air support system used so successfully in Khe Sanh defense.
>
> ....met Baig socially several years ago and invited him out to HQs for detailed debrief on Khe Sanh's operation. He is very imaginative military professional with touches of real brilliance. He is also quite unique in many respects....
>
> Baig has been advised informally through USMC channels that quote friends of ...... unquote will be contacting him to talk about techniques of air support. Suggest that through...... you get in touch with him to pick his fertile brain. We recognize, as would he, that Khe Sanh quite different situation from Ban Na but we believe he could provide some very useful and practical suggestion. End of message.

Carver's cable-request may have resulted in even heavier bombing by B-52's in Operation *Lam Son 719*, and the North Vietnamese may have "sent a message" to the U.S. regarding violation of the 1952 Geneva accords.

George Herring, Professor Emeritus at the University of Kentucky, described the Vietnam War as follows:

Aftermath

The years 1963 – 1973 were a time of paradox and confusion. The United States moved haltingly toward detente with the Soviet Union and rapprochement with China. At the same time, it drastically escalated and became bogged down in what one U.S. official aptly called an all-out limited war in Vietnam—a war fought, ironically, in the name of a Cold War that seemed to be winding down. Throughout these years, Vietnam and detente intersected in important and often contradictory ways. Although the Sino-Soviet split was out in the open by 1965 and the United States was pursuing detente with the Soviet Union, fear that the Saigon government might fall led President Johnson to initiate bombing of North Vietnam and dispatch of U.S. combat troops to South Vietnam.

These decisions reflected a rising fear of China, now seen as the major Cold War adversary. They were also based on reflexive Cold War beliefs that if the U.S. did not uphold its commitments, its credibility would be fatally undermined, making containment of China and detente with the USSR more difficult. Just as Cold War exigencies seemed to require an expanded U.S. commitment to South Vietnam, they drove China and the Soviet Union to back North Vietnam. In fact, given their raging competition for leadership of world communism, neither could let the other gain an edge in this regard. The aid provided by China and the Soviet Union was substantial and helped to ensure North Vietnam's ultimate victory. In this sense, the Vietnam War also posed a barrier to detente.

The United States, China, and the Soviet Union also feared that their involvement in Vietnam might threaten escalation to a general, even nuclear war. Determined to avoid the disastrous mistakes of the Korean conflict, both communist powers worked secretly with the United States to limit the possibility of further escalation. Also remembering Korea, the United States assured Beijing through secret contacts that it would not threaten China's border.

In the United States especially, the Vietnam War also ultimately increased pressures for detente. By the late 1960s, that war dominated the nation's foreign policy and political discourse. It triggered a sharp economic downswing, and by 1968 the worst economic crisis since the Great Depression.

Dissent Outcomes

The War Planning Strategy 1965. The President, Secretary of Defense, and Chairman of the Joint Chiefs of Staff avoided making a realistic estimate of force levels, likely duration, and

Courageous Dissent

potential casualties of the Vietnam War. General Wallace Greene, Commandant of the Marine Corps, disagreed and stated his opinion directly to the President and to the other members of the Joint Chiefs. General Greene's estimate of the costs of the Vietnam War was extraordinarily accurate. In the two weeks leading up to President Johnson's Press Conference on 28 July 1965, General Greene specifically and accurately estimated the force levels and war duration in Vietnam: 500,000 troops for five years. At that Press Conference, the President said: "I have ordered today...to raise our fighting strength from 75,000 to 125,000." Two days later on 30 July, the Joint Chiefs of Staff estimated 298,000 troops. On 7 December 1965, Secretary McNamara recommended 400,000 troops. On 16 December 1965, the Commander in Chief, Pacific sent revised requirements for 443,000 troops. Force levels in Vietnam actually increased from 125,000 to 443,000 troops in five months. President Johnson ignored General Greene's advice. To imply a requirement of a force level of 125,000 troops was false and unethical. Being lied to by the President tainted the public trust, and in the coming years, Americans became "war-weary," and insisted on ending the war.

The Warfighting Strategy 1966. Lt General Krulak expressed his dissent in a 19-page paper titled "Strategic Appraisal," discussing it first with the chain of command, and finally with the President in the Oval Office in August 1966. "Attrition was the route to defeat ...the Vietnamese people are the prize...our self-declared victories in the search-and-destroy operations are not relevant to the total outcome of the war." Secretary of Defense McNamara and President Johnson ignored General Krulak and supported the attrition/search-and-destroy approach advocated by General Westmoreland. When the US abandoned the attrition strategy in 1968 and implemented a comprehensive warfighting strategy that included pacification, it was too late.

The Barrier Strategy 1967. The anti-infiltration Barrier proposal was the idea of Secretary of Defense McNamara and was opposed by nearly every military leader in the chain of command - including every Marine General and the Navy Commander in the Pacific. The most specific and detailed objection to the barrier was delivered at the Barrier Study Conference in October 1966: Before construction began in 1967, the plans for the DMZ barrier were disputed three times by the future "owner" of the barrier—General Kyle, Commanding General of the 3rd Marine Division. His dissent consisted of a detailed "Non-Concur" report, followed by presentations to the Commandant of the Marine Corps and Assistant Secretary of the Navy. Approved by Secretary McNamara in 1966, the anti-infiltration barrier would be canceled less than three years later. In 1969, Defense Secretary Melvin Laird testified to Congress that the original barrier plan "did not work out as expected."

The Strong Point Strategy/Defending Khe Sanh 1968. Like the Barrier proposal, Marine military leaders opposed the defense of Khe Sanh. In 1966, General Westmoreland asked the Marines to conduct a war game to analyze the defense of northern I Corps and was briefed by the Marines on the results of that war game. "I notice you haven't made any comment about putting a force in Khe Sanh. What's your reason for this?" said General Westmoreland. The Marines' response was a defense line west from Dong Ha to the Rock Pile. They recommended against attempting to hold anything north of Route 9 nor to defend to the west of Route 9, where Khe Sanh was located. Khe Sanh was too isolated, too hard to support, and it would be easy for the NVA to cut Highway 9, assuming it could be opened. Eventually, the Marines complied with General Westmoreland and agreed to defend Khe Sanh. The clearest dissent to the decision to defend Khe Sanh was voiced by Marine Brigadier General Lowell English in January 1967, one year before the siege of Khe Sanh began. The 1968 defense of Khe Sanh was a terrible decision, resulting in nearly one thousand lost lives.

The High Mobility Strategy/Operation Dewey Canyon 1969. This one good decision was to violate the order to man strong points across the DMZ. U.S. Marine Major General Ray Davis re-oriented the 3rd Marine Division along the high-mobility tactics that had been demonstrated by the U.S. Army in Operation *Pegasus*. General Davis sought and received permission from his commanders to violate the McNamara Line concept. Davis recommended that forward positions where a battalion had been "holed up" would have only one company each; the other three rifle companies would deploy as a mobile force to seek out the enemy. As part of this change in tactics, Davis ordered Operation *Dewey Canyon* in the A Shau Valley. Operation *Dewey Canyon* was not a search-and-destroy operation aimed at NVA forces. It was a regimental-sized raid aimed at NVA logistics along the Laos border. Together, Davis and his U.S. Army commanders successfully dissented the McNamara line concept. The results of Operation *Dewey Canyon* in 1969 were described by U.S Army Lt Gen. Richard Stilwell as "unparalleled and deserves space in American military history."

In the words of Secretary James Mattis, these five dissenters were all "entrusted with the lives of our troops, and with enormous sums of taxpayer money." In our view, their dissent was ethical. Regrettably, they were ignored 80% of the time.

Conclusion

The U. S. withdrawal from South Vietnam was a catastrophic defeat. The cost in lives was over 58,000 American KIA and more than one million South East Asian lives lost. That loss was felt by those who lived through the Vietnam era, those that lost relatives and loved ones, and Vietnam veterans that experienced the war firsthand. Sadly, some costs of the Vietnam War are still evident today, including post-traumatic stress disorder (PTSD), Agent Orange, and lives that were shortened by that conflict. Bad decisions made from 1965 to 1968 contributed to the pursuit of warfare strategies that were principal contributors to America's failure.

Perhaps the only positive legacy of the Vietnam War was described by Lee Quon Yew, President of Singapore. Lee wrote to President Lyndon Johnson that the U.S. war in Vietnam bought time to stabilize Southeast Asian governments and economies. Malaysian Prime Minister Tunku Abdul Rahman supported the U.S. war in Vietnam and succeeded in winning more American investment in his country. Thai military elites, including Prime Minister Thanon Kittikakorn, aligned Thailand with America from 1950 onward. Indonesia's President Sukarno claimed to be non-aligned and sought foreign assistance from all the Cold War powers. None of their countries in Southeast Asia—Singapore, Malaysia, Thailand, or Indonesia—fell under the control of China or the USSR.

The actions of the Marine Generals—including their dissent—form an important picture of warfighting in the Vietnam War during five critical years. Baig's life provides a picture of the combat experience that most Vietnam veterans knew. The combination of different kinds of stories—family lives, and military operations—are needed for a full appreciation of the impact that the Vietnam War had on America.

General Wallace Greene's final assignment was Commandant of the Marine Corps. During his 37-year career, Greene

Aftermath

gained a reputation as a brilliant staff officer, long-range planner, and troubleshooter. Greene died (age 95) in 2003.

Lieutenant General Victor Krulak's final assignment was Fleet Marine Force Pacific. After retiring from the Marine Corps, Krulak worked for Copley Newspapers, including serving as president of Copley News Service and vice president of Copley Press. Krulak died in 2008 (age 95) in San Diego, CA.

Major General Wood Kyle's final assignment was the command of the 5th Marine Division in Camp Pendleton, CA. Kyle retired in 1968, after 32 years of military service. Following his retirement, he worked for a defense contractor in the Bay Area of California. Kyle died in 2000 (age 85) in Oceanside, CA.

Major General Lowell English's final assignment was Commanding General, Marine Corps Recruit Depot, San Diego, California. He retired from the Marine Corps in 1969, after 31 years of commissioned service. English accepted a job as the director of the San Diego Museum of Man, serving in that capacity for ten years until 1982. English died in 2005 (age 90) in San Diego, CA.

Major General Davis returned to the U.S. and served as director, Education Center, Marine Corps Development and Education Command, Quantico, Virginia. Following his 1970 promotion to Lieutenant General and serving as Commanding General, Marine Corps Development and Education Command, Davis was promoted to the grade of general and became Assistant Commandant of the Marine Corps. He was advised privately that the Pentagon was recommending him to be Commandant; however, he was aware of the personal preference of President Nixon for a different Marine. The White House told the Pentagon not to submit any recommendations, and General Davis was passed over for the position of Commandant of the Marine Corps. General Ray Davis retired from the Marine Corps in 1972. Davis died in 2003 (age 88) in Conyers, Georgia.

Thirty-nine-year-old Major Mirza Baig USMC, his thirty-one-year-old wife Diane Helene, and their nine-year-old daughter Juliette Cecile were buried at Arlington National Cemetery, following a service at Ft. Myer Chapel on 4 May 1971. Their graves are three miles from St Matthews' Cathedral, where Mirza and Diane had been married eleven years before.

The Baig family had been asleep in their rooms on the fourth floor of the Imperial Hotel in Bangkok, Thailand when a fire broke out from an overheated grill, which in turn ignited grease

The Baig Tombstone in Arlington Cemetery. Mirza is on the front face of the stone and his wife Diane and daughter Cecile are listed on the back of the stone.

and bottled cooking gas. Flames quickly entered the ventilation/air conditioning system. The fire escape doors at each end of the corridor had been bolted shut from the outside.

Doctors at the U.S. Army Field Hospital outside Bangkok said that most of the victims were Americans. Police said they had recovered 22 bodies and expected to find more. The Imperial was a modern, 110-room hotel, located in Bangkok's diplomatic quarter, frequented by U.S. diplomats, military officers, and their families, as well as tourists of various nationalities. Some of the survivors complained that no alarm was sounded, the firemen were late, and the fire escapes were difficult to find in the confusion of darkness, smoke, and fire. The Baig family was staying at the hotel while awaiting final orders to return to the Second Marine Division in Camp Lejeune, N.C., reporting to General Tompkins. "My friend and I were oblivious to anything else going on except doing what we could to get the people out of there," said Lt. Colonel Gene Leupp, who was on leave from his U.S. Air Force station in Hawaii. "The pity is, I couldn't find a fire escape. There must be one, but I couldn't find it."

Aftermath

The Baig family funeral was attended by several Generals who served with Baig in Vietnam: including Robert Cushman, then Deputy Directory of the CIA, and Rathvon Tompkins, base commander in Camp Lejeune, NC. That evening, the Baig family including Ambassador Mirza Baig, his wife Juliette, and son Taimur were invited to dinner at the home of the Commandant of the Marine Corps at Marine barracks, 8th & I St, Washington D.C. During the dinner, General Chapman, then Commandant of the Marine Corps, expressed his feelings and those of the many Marines who had known "Harry." "Mrs. Baig, you have lost a son, but we have lost a special Marine."

Baig was awarded a second Legion of Merit: "His contributions...were of extraordinary benefit to the Royal Thai Government. The Prime Minister of Thailand officially request(ed) Major Baig's normal tour of duty extended." Baig's friend, Captain Kent Steen USMC wrote, "With the perspective of age, I realize the Marine Corps attracts strongly put together people, but Harry was clearly of another genius... I was more aware than most how near [i.e., tenuous] a thing our survival was... he couldn't get enough credit... Harry was one of a kind."

)( )(

Courageous Dissent

Appendices

Appendix A

Commandant Greene's Memorandums,
July 1965

The original copies of his Memorandum to file for the 15 July 1965 HASC meeting and the 22 July White House SEA Conference are kept at the US Marine Corps University Library in Quantico, VA

**DEPARTMENT OF THE NAVY
HEADQUARTERS UNITED STATES MARINE CORPS
WASHINGTON. D.C. 20310**

MEMORANDUM FOR THE RECORD
Subj: First Meeting of Joint Chiefs of Staff with Policy Subcommittee of The House Armed Services Committee, 150730July1965

1. The meeting was held in the Office of the Chairman (Mr. L. Mendel Rivers) in Room 2118 RHOB. Present were:
CJCS (Chairman JCS, General Wheeler was not present due to the fact that he had departed at 2000 on Thurs, 14Jul, with SecDef and party for an inspection trip to SVN)
CNO - Admiral McDonald (Acting Chairman JCS)
C/S USA - General Johnson
C/S USAF - General McConnell
CMC - General Greene

Chairman HASC - Mr. L. Mendel Rivers (D S.Car)
Ranking Minority Leader- William H. Bates (R Mass)
Mr. F. Edward Hebert (D La)
Mr. Phillip J. Philbin (D Mass)
Mr. Melvin Price (D Ill)
Mr. John R. Blandford, Chief Counsel

2. Mr. RIVERS stated that this was the first of a series of regularly scheduled meetings that the Policy Subcommittee of

Appendices

the HASC planned to hold with the Joint Chiefs of Staff. A schedule of the meetings will be provided the Joint Chiefs in the near future.

3. The following subjects were discussed.
A. MOBILIZATION. Is mobilization necessary to meet the personnel requirements in the escalating situation in South Vietnam?

The Chairman asked each of the Chiefs and the CMC how many people they each felt would be required for his own Service. I stated that the Marine Corps had an immediate requirement for approximately 14,000 officers and enlisted men and that if the situation continued to escalate and more Marine Corps forces were required, that the Marine Corps would then need approximately 150,000 more officers and enlisted. I pointed out to the Chairman that at the present time we had some 28,000 Marines committed to South Vietnam with portions of the 1st Marine Division committed, in addition to the 3d Marine Division/1st Wing Team; that we have been able to establish (1) three secure areas-these secure areas in I CORPS, that in my opinion was desirable to join these secure areas into an amphibious coastal enclave as soon as possible, and that if it were to be done, it would require at least 150,000 more officers and men for the Marine Corps. I pointed out the advantages of this course of action. The NAVY indicated that their requirement would be 40,000 additional men. McDONALD did not indicate whether this was an immediate requirement or a full escalation effort. General JOHNSON wandered around in his discussion for several minutes indicating in essence that he didn't really know what his requirement was, either for today or in the future. However after repeated questions from the Chairman, he came up with a figure of 200,000 or 250,000 as the Army's requirement, which I thought to mean was based on a full escalation effort. General MCCONNELL attempted to answer for the Air Force in terms of aircraft squadrons which would have to be moved forward and he was vague as to the exact number of men that the Air Force would require. He mentioned several figures, all below 100,000. The inevitable deduction that the Committee members must have made was that mobilization was going to be necessary if a political settlement could not be reached. Near the end of the discussion, the Chairman asked me how many men I felt would be required to cope with the situation overall in South

Courageous Dissent

Vietnam, and I replied that my estimate was at least 500,000 U.S. troops would be required. No reaction to this statement was evidenced by any member of the Committee or by the Joint Chiefs.

B. CIVIC ACTION. I discussed the Civic Action Program in I-CORPS area pointing out the benefits particularly in the intelligence field which came natives realized we were their friends and wanted to help them.

C. COMBINED OPERATIONS. The Chairman stated that he felt the only way our operations could succeed in South Vietnam was by integrating the South Vietnamese into U.S. Forces. He stated that this was what had been done with the "Niggers" during World War II and Korea and this was what we must do with the South Vietnamese. General JOHNSON immediately spoke out against this idea stating that our experience in Korea had been due to the language difficulty when the Koreans were actually integrated with U. S. troops - they wound up doing "lifting and hauling" jobs; i.e. hewers of wood and bearers of water. I came in at this point (2) and described the combined operations which were placed in I-CORPS area, and which were proving to be highly successful. I pointed out that this integration was not on a man-for-man basis but consists of a Vietnamese unit of a platoon or larger size, working' directly with similar U. S. units under single commander. I gave the example of Popular Force Platoons which were working with U. S. Marines and had become so integrated and with Marine Corps spirit that many of them wore Marine Corps emblems on their collars or caps.

D. ACTIONS IN NORTH VIETNAM. Mr. RIVERS produced a map from a locked closet - the map was labeled SECRET and had some marks on it indicating how the harbor of HAIPHONG could be mined. The chart was actually a nautical chart of Haiphong and its harbor. "Why weren't we mining Haiphong Harbor or bombing the tremendous POL storage sites in the vicinity?" asked the Chairman and Mr. BLANDFORD. "Haven't you Chiefs recommended that this be done?" I sat silent and let Admiral McDONALD and General MCCONNELL reply to this. Both of them stated that these targets had been among many others on a recommended list, but that no time had been set for an attack on these Haiphong targets. "Political factors entered into the decision as to when Haiphong should be attacked because, said Admiral McDonald, "many of our Allies and free world countries have ships entering Haiphong Harbor to trade with the North Vietnamese and we don't want to do anything at this time which would alienate these allies of ours. "

Mr. BLANDFORD asked why the large bridge over the river near Haiphong was not bombed, because a great deal of POL products, over 600 tons a day, was being brought into the city over this bridge. He received the same answer as had just been previously given regarding attacks on Haiphong Harbor. These answers in my opinion were not truthful in that the POL target at Haiphong had been recommended several times for attack under the "ROLLING THUNDER PROGRAM" and had been turned down by the SECDEF or the WHITE HOUSE. The Chairman then asked why the SAM sites and IL-28's around HANOI had not been struck.

He addressed this question specifically to me and my reply was that I had been greatly concerned about the L-28s from the day they had first appeared in North Vietnam and that I had been equally worried about the SAM sites from the day the first shovel had been struck into the ground by the North Vietnamese to initiate site construction. (3)

E. A minimum of 500,000 U.S. troops to be required in South Vietnam.

F. An immediate intensification of operations in Northern and South Vietnam (i.e., bombing of many of the targets which have not been bombed as yet and some of which were discussed during the morning's meeting).

Mr. HEBERT then spoke about the role of the Joint Chiefs of Staff and reinforced the statement the Committee Chairman had previously made in which he said the Committee were friends of the Chiefs and wanted to do whatever was necessary to provide the proper military forces for the Country. Mr. HEBERT pointed out that the chiefs were highly respected, and that if they were to continue in this status they would have to provide the Committee with their opinions without fear or favor. At this moment the chairman chimed in with the statement "The Chiefs were creatures of the Congress and had a duty to them as well as to the Executive Branch." General JOHNSON immediately responded to these statements by inviting the Committee's attention to the fact that the National Security Act of 1957 specifically outlined the duties of the Joint Chiefs, making them solely advisors to the President, the National Security Council, and the Secretary of Defense. I immediately bolstered this statement by saying that as a result of this law, which Congress itself had made, the Chiefs were required to provide advice to the President and the Secretary of Defense and that if this advice and recommendation was not accepted by the President and the Secretary of Defense when the Joint Chiefs and the Commandant were called over — as they were this morning to consult with the Committee — the Chiefs found themselves in a very difficult position between the Committee and the Administration. Mr. BATES immediately spoke up and said, "That Law is the worst one that Congress ever passed."

4. The Committee broke up at 0810, and not feeling like eating any of Mr. River's coffee and doughnuts I went home to eat some breakfast before going on to the office.

5. After arriving at HQMC and at 1030, I had the Military Secretary get in touch with Mr. BLANDFORD by phone and I then gave BLANDFORD the following six items which I said represented the situation as I saw it this morning. Unless a political solution to the situation in South Vietnam is reached immediately, the following things will result:
- A major war between the U. S. and the communist side
- A campaign of several years-at least five
- A large number of casualties for the United States
- A general mobilization in the U. S. in the immediate offing (4)
- A minimum of 500,000 U.S. troops to be required in South Vietnam
- An immediate intensification of operations in North and South Vietnam (i. e., bombing of many of the targets which have not been bombed as yet and some of which were discussed during the morning's meeting)

My general impression this morning was that the Committee found themselves in fit of frustration. They are unable to get the information which they want from the WHITE HOUSE or from the SECDEF, and they are trying to secure this information from the Chiefs, well knowing that in doing so they are placing the Chiefs in an extremely difficult position. Between the Committee and the Administration (President and SECDEF). I am also certain from watching the actions of the Chiefs that they have no intention of placing themselves in a position where they can be damaged by either the Committee, the President, or the SECDEF. In other words there is not going to be any frank exchange of information with the Committee nor will any recommendations for action be proposed to the Committee which are contrary to decisions or positions already established by the WHITE HOUSE or the SECDEF. Furthermore I was astounded by how few of the facts regarding the actual situation seemed to be known to the Chairman or his members. The Chairman also discussed at some length with a little assistance from Mr. HEBERT the advisability of going forward with the amalgamation of the National Guard and the Reserve Forces of the Army. Apparently they wanted General JOHNSON to say that it wasn't a good idea in view of the current emergency. But, JOHNSON wouldn't say this, instead he replied that he felt it was a good idea and that the plan for amalgamation should continue in spite of the situation which existed in Southeast Asia.(5)

WALLACE M. GREENE, JR.
General, U. S. Marine Corps
Commandant of the Marine Corps

DEPARTMENT OF THE NAVY
HEADQUARTERS UNITED STATES MARINE CORPS
WASHINGTON. D.C. 20310

MEMORANDUM FOR THE RECORD
Subj: Record of Conference on Southeast Asia held at White House; 221150July1965

PRESENT:
Secretary of Defense	McNAMARA
Under SecDef	VANCE
Chairman JCS	WHEELER
Secretary	ZUCKERT, and his relief BROWN
Secretary USN	NITZE
Secretary USA	RESOR
C/S USA	JOHNSON
CNO	McDONALD
C/S USAF	McCONNELL
CMC	GREENE
White House Staff	McGeorge BUNDY
White House Staff	Bill D. MOYERS
White House Staff	Jack VALENTI
Chairman Foreign Intelligence Advisory Bd and Personal Advisor to President	Clark CLIFFORD

1. The meeting opened at 1150; the PRESIDENT had not yet arrived. However, the SECDEF commenced a discussion with those present regarding what the PRESIDENT wanted. McNAMARA stated that the 'PRESIDENT wanted to consider: (a) alternatives, and (b) will the selected alternative "win"? (or what will it accomplish?) The Secretary of the Navy inquired as to how the troops would be employed under the 34 Battalion (Westmoreland) Plan. "Are they to be used to attack the Viet Cong if the Viet Cong are in large concentrations? If the Viet Cong are not in large concentrations, will the U.S. troops be used to augment the RVN in pacification?" He then discussed the requirement for numbers of troops in area and stated that he had made a careful study of this requirement and felt that more would be required than allocated under the 34 Battalion Plan. Having made his statement, SECNAV turned to me, and I agreed that what he had said was correct and that I felt that 100,000 troops (and I meant U.S.) would be required to carry

Appendices

out the operation which had been initiated in 1-CORPS. The SECDEF immediately replied that the total number of troops required should include all third country and RVN troops that would be available in I-CORPS area. Westmoreland wanted 175,000 U.S. troops added to RVN available. U.S. troops would be used to hit the Viet Cong, if we can find them in large numbers — if not, then in pacification. It is not clear as to whether we would be successful in pacification. The question is, can we guarantee that they can pacify? It is not clear that they can. The great uncertainty— how do you pacify the country? Previous plans haven't worked—haven't met the goal.

2. At 1200 the meeting was interrupted by the PRESIDENT who entered with the British Ambassador (Sir Patrick DEAN). He introduced those present to the Ambassador and then both left the room. At 1203 the meeting resumed and the discussion continued.The Chairman said that pacification depended on security and the people that Westmoreland wanted to establish secure base areas for 44 battalions and to establish a reaction (striking) Force. At this time (1204) the PRESIDENT re-entered the meeting. SECDEF stated that the Joint Chiefs had only had a short time to review the SECDEF's paper (SecDef Memorandum for the President, 20 July 1965, Top Secret) and, therefore, they were not prepared to discuss the requirements for call-up and budgetary matters however he recommended that the PRESIDENT ask for the Chiefs' views on alternatives (courses of action) and the possible results from these different alternatives. (The Secretary was referring to paragraph 4 of his memorandum, titled Options open to us. The PRESIDENT then said that he would like to have SECDEF or McGeorge BUNDY outline some of the problems involved in the alternatives.The SECDEF now outlined the courses of action as proposed in paragraph 4 of his memorandum. He indicated that his choice was paragraph 4c; i.e., to "Expand promptly and substantially the US military pressure against the Viet Cong in the South. " (see memo)

3. The PRESIDENT then as is typical of him at such meetings, proceeded to go around the table, individual by individual, asking each man for his views. He started with CNO SECNAV, USAF, Mr. ZUCKERT and Mr BROWN followed in that order. Not having arrived with an outline of my views, I stopped taking

notes and proceeded to put together an outline so that I would be ready to adequately express my ideas when my turn arrived. The PRESIDENT finally reached me and I started by saying: "Mr. President, these are my views and recommendations." I was seated at the far end of the table (east) facing inboard. The President interrupted me and said that he didn't have a hearing aid. I immediately replied, "Well, Mr. President I'll speak louder and make sure that you and everyone else in this room hears what I have to say because I welcome this opportunity to express my views and recommendations to you.

First, as regards the Situation South Vietnam. I consider it to be worse today than at any time in the past since we entered the country. However, the situation is not hopeless, and I am firmly convinced that we can find a solution to the problem which exists there if we are willing to pay the price. The first thing we have to do is to determine what our stakes are. I consider that these stakes fall in three categories. In order of importance, they are as follows:

First, our National Security Stake. I believe that if we were to withdraw from South Vietnam, we would simply be delaying a final accounting with the Communist side. By that, I mean that we would have to go into some other place such as MALAYA, THAILAND, INDIA, MIDDLE EAST, or if we delay long enough, even in LATIN AMERICA. And the longer we delay, the more it will cost when the final accounting takes place.

Our second stake is our Pledge to South Vietnam. I believe that this pledge should be honored. However, I also realize that there are a number of people in the United States who believe that we should welch on this pledge rather than to pay the price in money and casualties which it will take in order to permit us to honor the pledge.

The third stake is that of U. S. prestige before the rest of the world. To me this is an important factor also but here again many of our people do not feel that this is important enough to pay the price. I believe that the first and most important stake that of national security has not been realized by most of our people and l feel that if this is explained to them by you that the majority be willing to pay whatever it may take to win in South Vietnam. Assuming then that we are going to stay in South Vietnam, we should then turn to the Strategy necessary to win. I have divided strategy into two parts: (1) Strategy in South Vietnam, and (2) Strategy in North Vietnam. Insofar as strategy in South Vietnam is concerned, I feel that we have already demonstrated in I-CORPS area a method which will permit us to win. As you know, we have secured three coastal areas in I-CORPS. This has been done by putting 28,000 Marines ashore in that area. I feel that these three secure areas should be expanded into a single coastal enclave this can be done by the introduction of additional forces as rapidly as possible.

I believe that a total of 100,000 Marines two Divisions and one Wing will be necessary to establish this enclave. If this action is taken the lines of communication (i.e. the north-south railroad and the main north-south highway) can be secured and what is more important is that approximately 30% of all of the people in South Vietnam can be made secure within this enclave. I feel that this enclave technique can likewise be applied to the other three CORPS areas. I realize that because of the more unfavorable terrain conditions in the other CORPS areas that it will take more men and time to establish adequate enclaves. However I firmly believe that this method can be applied successfully to all four CORPS areas. In addition to this military strategy the Civil Action Program in FIRST CORPS area should also be considered. In fact, I believe this to be as important as the military action. At the present time Marines in I-CORPS are distributing food, clothing medical attention, and are rebuilding villages, bridges digging wells and performing other actions to help the villagers in the liberated enclave area. Through this action the people are becoming convinced that the Marines are there to help them and as a result, the people are turning over Viet Cong to the Marines, or telling the Marines where the Viet Cong forces are located. Now as to the strategy in the North, I agree with the Chief of Staff of the Air Force that we have not been successful there because we have not been hitting the right targets. As a specific example: I believe that the supplies which are large and located in the Port of Haiphong area should be destroyed. There are millions of gallons of fuel located in these storage areas and that fuel is being used in motor vehicles and for other purposes to carry the war against us in South Vietnam. Although I am an amateur at politics, I fail to understand why, when we know that at least one hardcore regular North Vietnamese Division is operating against our forces in South Vietnam, that we hesitate for political reasons to bomb the POL dumps near HANOI and HAIPHONG. I believe that this type of target can be destroyed with a minimum loss of civilian lives.

I also feel that the MIGS and IL-28's located on the in North Vietnam should be destroyed. Furthermore, when the SAM sites become operational, they should also be attacked. I believe that the bridges northwest of HANOI should be bombed and, finally the industrial targets; i.e., the factories and other industrial Installations which have taken the North Vietnamese ten years to develop, should be destroyed after the targets which I have just described have been hit.

Now I want to talk about another action which has not yet been discussed at this meeting, and that is a Blockade. I believe that the Port of HAIPHONG should be blockaded by the Navy and that if this is not feasible because of the location of the Communist-held HAINAN Island, that the Port of HAIPHONG should be mined in order to prevent the entry of supplies and equipment which are contributing to the Communist ability to carry on the war. I also propose Mr. President, a similar Blockade Action against CAMBODIA. During my recent trip to South Vietnam, I questioned a number of U. S. and South Vietnamese officers as I had done before, regarding the entry of war materials. Into South Vietnam via CAMBODIA. All of them felt that a great deal of material was being introduced through CAMBODIA. If you were to ask me here to prove this to you, I could not do so but I recommend that a blockade be established to determine just that and whether or not, for example, war materials are being brought in through the Port of SIHANOUKVILLE.

Now as to the time which will be required to win a victory in South Vietnam, I feel that it will take a minimum of 5 years and will require at least 500,000 U.S. troops.

And, lastly, Mr. President, based on my sampling the people in this Country during my various trips out of Washington, I am convinced that if you will tell the people what our stakes in South Vietnam are that the majority of them will back you in the action which I have just described."

4. I feel that this record of what I told the PRESIDENT is very important in establishing the Marine Corps position directly with him. As can be seen, the PRESIDENT made no effort to confine himself, as SECDEF had suggested, to the question solely of alternatives and whether or not a selected alternative would win. I watched the Secretary of Defense during this

Appendices

development, and I had the clear impression that he was not too happy over this turn of events.

Following my presentation, the PRESIDENT then called the Chief of Staff Army, who was sitting on my left. JOHNSON, as he usually does, held forth on the philosophical background behind U.S. actions in South Vietnam. He did not offer any specific recommendations as courses of action, and when the PRESIDENT asked him what he would do if the Chinese Communists were to enter the conflict on a large scale as a result of U.S. escalatory action, JOHNSON gave a vague reply to the effect that this would bring us to another stage at which point further decisions would have to be made. The PRESIDENT next called on the new Secretary of the Army, Mr. RESOR. Mr.RESOR attempted to take the somewhat noncommittal approach that BROWN had taken before him saying that he had not been Secretary for very long and he therefore was not really prepared to offer any detailed recommendations. The PRESIDENT immediately challenged him on this saying he was the Secretary of the Army and was attending this meeting for the purpose of advising the PRESIDENT, and that in later years a story was to be written about this meeting, which the whole Country was watching today a story similar to that about the "Bay of Pigs" which was appearing now in the daily papers — the PRESIDENT wanted to make sure that the views of everyone present would be known. Secretary RESOR made no reply at this time but about 10 minutes later during the general discussion which followed Secretary RESOR interrupted the conversation and asked permission to state his views. RESOR said that he recommended that Westmoreland's proposal be approved and that additional troops be introduced at the rate asked for. "This was Mr. McNAMARA's plan also, said RESOR (apparently watching his P's and Q's with his job)."Our prestige was at stake, said Mr. RESOR, "in Thailand and other places. RESOR said he felt that after the first of the year additional forces would have to be introduced. "Our (U.S.) people must be patient while the pressure is on."

5. During the entire meeting, OKAMURA, the Presidential Photographer circled around the as he usually does, taking many pictures of the meeting.

6. The PRESIDENT asked McGeorge BUNDY to summarize for those present all of the criticisms and arguments that would be brought against the PRESIDENT if he appeared before the Congress with a proposal that would require the commitment of "millions of American boys" for a period of years in Southeast Asia. "Why", said the PRESIDENT, "if I were to do this, mothers would come out of their pantries and take their aprons off!" This remark did not indicate to me that the PRESIDENT did not believe that we should not stay in South Vietnam and increase our effort there. The PRESIDENT did not indicate what his decision was going to be. He thanked us for our comments and recommendations and said that he, alone, would have to make the decision as to what we should do and that he would be a "lonely man" in arriving at the decision point.

WALLACE M. GREENE, JR.
General, U. S. Marine Corps
Commandant of the Marine Corps

Appendix B

A Strategic Appraisal Vietnam
December 1965

Lt. Gen. Victor J. Krulak's Strategic Appraisal

A STRATEGIC APPRAISAL VIETNAM

I. Introduction.
The U.S. effort in Southeast Asia today is great and growing steadily greater. It represents vast logistic power and substantial military strength, promising soon to approach that which we committed in Korea. Our casualties, not yet great by Korean war standards, are growing nevertheless, and the gross burden on the United States becomes more onerous with each passing day.

Historically, the United States has not recoiled from sacrifice in war, particularly as the object could be seen and the strategy understood. Indeed, the only adverse public reactions to war in this century have occurred in the latter days of Korea, and again today, in each of which cases citizens found it hard to appreciate the military strategy, to visualize the route from where we are to where we want to go.

In the present case, the lack of understanding of what our military strategy is derives from the fact that it has never really been articulated. However, if it were to be described, it would have to be in about these terms:

"Attrit the enemy to a degree which makes him incapable of prosecuting the war, or unwilling to pay the cost of so doing".

If this is indeed the basis for our strategy, it has to be regarded as inadequate, even though it has generated limited progress in recent months. The paragraphs to follow seek to develop a more dynamic alternative, on the assumption that achievement of our objectives by political means—obviously to be preferred—is not successful, and that military action alone is required.

II. The Theater.

Geography and Meteorology. The general military geography of the Southeast Asia peninsula (Laos, North and South Vietnam, Cambodia) has come to be reasonably well understood. However a few essentials, which affect our strategy directly, may merit being underscored again.—not over twenty percent of the whole area is cultivated. The remainder is forest; much of which is very dense. Of the cultivation, fully eighty percent is in rice. The Mountains are high and rugged, extending in an almost unbroken chain from Yunnan, in China, to Nha Trang in South Vietnam. Altitudes reach 9000 feet and, within 35 miles of Nha Trang, are 7000 feet high. Military cross-country trafficability is poor, and the limited road system is subject to ready interdiction. The weather is always bad in Vietnam, at some point in the country. It is best, all around, in the early spring. The worst time for military operations in the Mekong Delta is in mid-summer, when there are about 12 inches of rain per month. It is worst in the central high-lands in late summer, with 15-18 inches of rain per month. It is worst in the Northern littoral in the autumn and early winter, with 20-30 inches per month. The most rain is found, not in the Mekong Delta as might be expected, but in the Hue-Danang region.

Population. There are more people in North Vietnam than in South Vietnam (18 million versus 15 million). In North Vietnam almost 90 per cent of the people are squeezed into Tonkin (the Red River basin) where the rural population goes as high as 3000 per square mile. Hanoi has some 750,000 people; Haiphong 370,000. In South Vietnam the population is concentrated in Saigon and the Mekong Delta (8 million) and along the coastal littoral from Hue to somewhere South of Nha Trang (4 million).

Politics. This is not the place for a comprehensive political analysis, but there is one political fact affecting directly the military strategy which is often forgotten. It is this: the people of South Vietnam really have no politics. A great generalization, this is nevertheless a fair one, if one regards politics as extending to the national—or even provincial—level. Except for the Montagnards, whose interests are tribal, the people are interested in their family, their hamlet or their village, and that is all. While they may participate in electing their village elders, they have little loyalty to, and less comprehension of, anything beyond this narrow horizon.

It has been said that "The National Liberation Front speaks for sixty per cent of the people in South Vietnam. " This may be so, but whatever speaking the Front does is certainly without the acquiescence, the understanding—or even the knowledge—of the great majority of the people involved.

And much the same is true for the relationship of the people and the Vietnamese government. It is doubtful if one villager in a thousand has ever heard of Premier Ky, or who even knows who his own Province Chief is. Ngo Dinh Diem understood this and made a mighty effort to extend to the villager an identification with a central government. He was indefatigable in visiting the countryside and talking with the people. Hundreds of thousands of lithographs of his picture were distributed in the hinterland, and were identified, at every turn, with government assistance to the people. Even so, and in eight years, Diem was able to make only a small dent in the amazing Vietnamese provincialism;--and that dent has largely disappeared now, simply by default.

This fact is important to development of a military strategy, because it is these same simple, provincial people who are the battlefield on which the war must be fought. Their provincialism is exploited by the VC at every turn. Not enough---not nearly enough--is being done to give the people a feel for or identity with a strong central government.

Religion. The canard that 90 per cent of all Vietnamese are Buddhists has largely been disproved, and it is now pretty well accepted that not over 20 per cent of the country is truly Buddhist. The bulk of the people reflect 1000 years of Chinese rule, in their leaning toward Confucianism and Taoism, while there is a healthy salting of Cao Dai, Hoa Hao and Moslems in the country, plus 10-15 per cent Christians. However, there occasionally recurs the apprehension that Vietnam may be "headed for another religious crisis" by virtue of Buddhist unrest. This, of course, could affect the military situation.

The fact is the hard-core Buddhist hierarchy is overwhelmingly involved in politics. They are well organized and, at any time, can create unrest if they choose. A good example was the recent flurry generated by the alleged damaging of a religious figure in a pagoda near Danang. The local bonzes wanted restitution, apology and assurance of non-recurrence. However, it turned out that they were not empowered to accept these gestures when proffered, until approval was received from Saigon.

Courageous Dissent

Thich Tri Quang, with too much communist association in his background for our good, can be expected to cause trouble when it suits his purpose. These facts are important in the contemplation of strategy, mainly as they underscore the need, as a matter of first business, for us to earn the trust and loyalty of the people; --people who can be and often are misguided, to the disadvantage of our effort, as was the case in the politically inspired Buddhist problems of 1963.

Economics. Outside the cities, fully 70 per cent of the people are involved in rice culture--either for subsistence or for livelihood. Rice is not everything, but in the eyes of the people, whose subsistence staple it is, rice plenty is synonymous with prosperity. And rice means rice fields--land; and land, being very near the heart of the people's part in the Vietnam War, is thus critical to our strategy.

In the pre-1954 years the absentee landlords wrung maximum tribute from the peasants; all the rent that the traffic would bear, usurious interest rates, and nothing at all in return. The farmer was squeezed between the needs of his own bare subsistence and the cupidity of the faceless landlord who spent his time in Saigon or on the Riviera.

The thousands of farmers who were living in virtual peonage were fertile ground for the communists to plough. They urged the peasants not to pay the rent at all and promised them that under communist rule the land would be forever theirs. Sometimes, in areas dominated by the Viet Cong (or Vietminh), they actually distributed some of the leaseholds, and provided spurious deeds to give the transfer a semblance of formality. Fortunately for us, the communist forces needed rice to support their military effort, and it has to come from this same land. Consequently, they soon were found exacting rice tribute from the same peasants, in a degree which made them not much more popular than the landlords.

When Ngo Dinh Diem was premier under Emperor Bao Dai and perceiving the depth to which the land problem affected the country's stability, he sought to promote some limited land reform, without success. However, when he became President he procured the passage of laws which put a limit on rents as well as on the amount of land that a landlord could own (some 113 hectares). Following passage of this law Diem initiated a program of buying surplus land from the landlords and distributing it, in small fee-simple parcels, to peasants. He also intended to

Appendices

redistribute expropriated French land, but that program was scarcely started when he was deposed. All in all, Diem had a fine idea, but it never got past the pilot stage, and succeeding governments have done little or nothing to carry it forward. The whole program is now largely ineffective.

So, the problem of land reform remains. The communists are still urging the peasants not to pay their rent and taxes—secretly looking ahead to the day when all the peasants will be communized, and all the land will be collectivized. The peasants are thus still squeezed between the needs of the government for taxes, the desires of the landlords for rent, and the extortionate pressures of the communists for rice and tribute.

All of this is central to our military campaign, because the war is not going to be won unless and until the peasants believe that the GVN--not the communists--is going to give them meaningful land reform. And this will require far more action than we have yet seen- action in the form of distribution of fee simple land, and in the form of some measure of relief for past unpaid taxes.

Without this we will not have the support of the countryside, which is to say we will not have the popular intelligence that is absolutely essential to winning the guerrilla battle. But if we can gain the rural support, we will gain with it not only the intelligence we require but will increasingly deny to the enemy the rice he needs to support his growing manpower investment as he pursues his strategy in RVN.

III. The Enemy Strategy.

No strategy is likely to be much of a success unless it takes departure from a decent knowledge of who the enemy is, what his object is, and how it is estimated that he is going about achieving his purposes.

In this area we enjoy great advantages, since the communists have announced exactly what they propose to do, and exactly how they are going about it. There is no mystery or doubt, as is often the case in war. Hitler, for instance, was sure we were going to land on the continent, but he had no clue as to whether it would be in Brittany, Normandy or elsewhere. However, in Vietnam we know the enemy strategy and tactics exactly; we know where he is planning to go and how he proposes to get there. He has told us. In his own terms, this is the way the enemy intends to bring the people and resources of South Vietnam under his control.

First, he acknowledged that the people are the target and, by use of trained political cadre, he seeks to subvert the villagers; propagandizing them in terms of promised land reform, no taxes, prosperity and a peaceful life. This has been going on for over a decade. Now it has come to include propaganda relating to U. S, imperialism, aimed at equating U. S. forces with the French, whom the peasants resented deeply, as being all take and no give.

Second, and in coordination with the subversive effort, he is waging a guerrilla war on the people, seeking to subdue them by terrorism and murder, while extorting their resources and sapping their substance by taxation and by kidnapping their youth for recruitment.

Third, he is seeking to erode the strength of the GVN regular and paramilitary forces, by ambush, localized attack and entrapment. His objective here is the GVN manpower base, which is fragile. By attacking it he hopes to draw as many as possible of the limited GVN forces away from the more productive task of protecting the people.

Finally, and latterly, he is seeking to attrit U.S. forces, through the process of violent, close-quarters combat which tends to diminish the effectiveness of our supporting arms. He hopes thus to inflict losses which will erode our national will and cause us to cease our support of the GVN. Giap never hoped to defeat the French on the battlefield, but he was sure that if the cost in casualties and francs was high enough, the French would defeat themselves in Paris. He was right. It is likely that he feels the same about the U.S.A.

There are several significant aspects of this four-part communist strategy. First, it will be noted that the overall formula focuses on people. At this juncture, and for the past 15 years, the communists have been struggling for minds, not territory. They are not interested in spilling their blood for hills or towns, nor are they interested in holding any ground except their jungle war zones--and they have been willing to relinquish some of these, on occasion, if the price for preserving them proved too high. Clearly, they feel that if they can possess the people, the territory will come along in good time.

Second, it will be noted that only two of the four concurrent elements of the enemy strategy involve direct contact with the prime target--the people. These are the subversive effort and the guerrilla war. The other two are peripheral to the central strategy; one aimed at degrading the capability of the GVN regular and paramilitary forces to interfere with the two prime actions, and the other aimed at degrading the will of the U. S, A, to help the GVN.

A key point here is this; the conflict between the PAVN/ hardcore VC on the one hand, and the U. S. on the other, could move to another planet today, and we would still not have won the war. On the other hand, if the subversion and guerrilla efforts were to disappear, the war would soon collapse, as the VC would be denied food, sanctuary, and intelligence.

The deductions generated by all of this are simply that: At all costs we must neutralize the subversion and comb the guerrillas out of the people's lives. And then we must protect the people, surely and continuously, in order that they may establish a strong society. This is the first and greatest task and justifies the commitment of whatever means are needed.

Concurrently, but only in those specific cases where intelligence shows the advantage to lie clearly with us, we should seize the initiative and attack their war zones on the ground. In any case, we should interdict the war zones continually from the air, at a level of violence which precludes their effective use for training and logistics.

Conversely, we must not engage in an attritional contest with the hard-core just for the sake of attrition; nor should we react to Viet Cong initiatives or seek them out just to do battle. The attritional ratio under these circumstances is not going to favor us, and this form of competition has little to do with who ultimately wins anyhow.

IV. The Reality of Attrition

At the outset it was observed that our current strategy pivots on attrition. Attrition, in turn, relates both to people and to material things; therefore, it will he worthwhile to recall again the essential truth that, in terms of people, the enemy's resources greatly exceed our own, while in material resources the exact reverse is true.

The combined Red Chinese/North Vietnamese military manpower pool is in excess of 100 million men. Ours and the South Vietnamese is not greater than 20 million. Admittedly, this ignores the peripheral manpower resources of Australia/

New Zealand and South Korea on the one hand, and of north Korea on the other; however these will not greatly alter the balance.

Thus, in the roughest of mechanical calculations, and contemplating total mobilization, we had better kill substantially more than five for one, or our attritional effort will lose ground, insofar as personnel resources are concerned.

But we are not doing anywhere near that well. Taking the period since the U. S. offensive effort has gained momentum, and under the most favorable terms, where we compare our own known dead and missing with our and GVN claims of enemy killed, we see that:

- In September, the kill ratio was 2.6 to 1 in our favor.
- In October, it was 2.8 to 1.
- In November, it was 2.6 to 1
- In December, it was 1.5 to 1

And it could very well be less favorable than these figures portray, since our estimates of enemy killed could be optimistic, and assumption that every dead body is, in fact, a VC may be too sanguine. But even if our figures are conservative; even if we were killing five--or even ten---for one, it would still require a great sacrifice in our own blood before the attritional effect came to be felt sufficiently by the enemy to bring him to conclude that he was over his head.

One criticism of the above line of reasoning is that it lumps the GVN and the U. S when we are not yet, in fact, confronted with Chinese volunteers. However, it would be imprudent not to credit the Chinese with the will to do what they were willing to do in Korea; to percolate their manpower into the battle, as needed, in order to make the attritional battle unprofitable to us. In any case, it would be a grave blow, were we to pursue the attritional program on the optimistic assumption that we and the GVN were matching manpower with the DRV alone, only to see an infusion of Chinese volunteers change the whole name of the game, after we had sacrificed many of our own lives.

A final point which must be mentioned respecting the Chinese factor is the possibility of our reacting with nuclear weapons, should Chinese soldiers appear on the Vietnam scene. Certainly, this would alter the whole equation. However, there are several pertinent questions in this regard. How many Chinese would we have to see in RVN before we took the great decision? How much would we have suffered in the interim? And

Appendices

what would we bomb in China in retaliation, besides the nuclear resources?

But even if the Chinese were not to put their manpower into the struggle, we had still best not undertake an attritional battle with the PAVN/VC, unless we are willing to mobilize completely, and to pay a substantial price in lives. Between the two-- DRV and VC, there is probably a military manpower pool of 2 1/2 million men. At the rate we are attriting them today, it will cost something like 175,000 U. S./GVN lives to reduce the enemy pool by only a modest 20 percent. At the present ratio, this means that, of the 175,000 killed, about 10,000 would be U. S. or, say, 60,000 U. S. casualties just to see the DRV/VC manpower resource degraded by 20 per cent, without any assurance that this would spell victory.

Turning to the material side of the attrition topic, the situation is potentially just the reverse, although not practically so at this time. The combined Chinese/DRV gross national product is about $50 billion. Ours, combined with the South Vietnamese, is not less than $650 billion. We make as much steel in a month as they do in a year. Our food production reflects a net annual surplus of 20 per cent, whereas they are hungry, undernourished countries, with food deficits. Beyond all this, our resources are far more flexible, far more adaptable to powerful application to the war effort.

For the communists to bring their material power to bear in South Vietnam demands a tremendous--and grossly inefficient— transportation effort. Furthermore, we know that, due to the accidents of geography, the enemy logistic system has vulnerable pressure points and is susceptible of interruption at the source. For instance, if no tanker ever entered Haiphong, Hong Gay or Vinh, and if no tank car ever ran on the rail lines between Hanoi and Red China, the DRV military effort would suffer a first magnitude blow. Crude though they are, VC and DRV operations heed POL to keep the battle moving, and, while there are other ways of importing fuel, the enemy would be hard put to make a go of it without the tankers or the tank cars. And this circumstance will intensify, as the DRV investment in SVN grows.

The same facts apply to other munitions. Fully three quarters of all munitions imports come into North Vietnam by sea. It is plain, however, that we are not now applying attrition-at-source, where it is most productive, but are seeking instead to intercept and destroy the enemy's material as it flows through the multiple channels of distribution, mainly through the Laos corridor. This, of course, is infinitely more difficult. While we have had some success to date in the armed reconnaissance role, it is plain that we have fallen far short of halting--or even gravely impeding--the flow. Nor has our effort given any evidence, as yet, of degrading the DRV determination.

All in all, our current material attrition program can be likened to fighting an alligator by chewing on his tail, well knowing that a shot between the eyes will be more effective, and far safer for you in the end. It has been said that attacks at the source (the main ports), attacks upon the major DRV stockpiles and attacks upon their heavy industry may be counterproductive, causing guerrilla retaliation on similar type installations in RVN.

The fact is, we should be acting now to prevent or defeat guerrilla attacks on the RVN power sources, POL storage and ports. If, as has been alleged, the communists have eschewed opportunities to damage major installations in the RVN, it is only because they judge that, by doing so, they stand to suffer more than we do. They are not likely to exercise forbearance as a sort of gentlemen's agreement when and if they feel it advantageous to do so, they will try to destroy the power plants, mine the Saigon River or blow up the ESSO tanks. Meanwhile, it would seem that we are surrendering initiative to them in an area where we are overwhelmingly superior.

In sum, and with respect only to the matter of attrition, there is good basis for concluding that a strategy built around manpower attrition promises us nothing but disappointment, whereas one which, among other things, emphasizes material attrition at the pressure points promises tangible benefit. This is not to suggest that the current and prospective commitments of U. S. forces are not necessary. They are simply because the GVN itself has neither the men nor the skill to do alone the many things that need to be done.

In the end, however, we are brought back to the acknowledgement that attrition alone cannot win the war, either by destroying the war machine or by applying graduated pressure to break the enemy's will. In both functions, attrition has a melancholy history and has disappointed its proponents. The Vietnam conflict ultimately has to be decided among the people in the villages of South Vietnam.

V. Winning the People.

In each of the preceding sections--one way or another--there has emerged the fact that the Vietnamese people are the prize. Much has been said about what should be done for them in terms of agrarian reform in order to win their allegiance and loyalty to an unbroken governmental chain stretching from the hamlet to Saigon. But land reform is not the whole story. As we compete with the communists for the popular loyalty there are other important battlegrounds;--health, education, agricultural improvements, transportation and communications.

In every one of these areas the GVN, with our help, can be infinitely superior to the communists, whose means for promoting popular betterment are limited. However, it has to be acknowledged that the GVN/U. S, program of bringing visible improvement to the lot of the peasant has gone forward far too slowly. The reasons are two-fold.

First, organization—the organization for pacification has been loose, diffuse and. inadequately supported at the top.--This goes for both the GVN and U. S, sides. There has been disagreement as to just what role the U. S, should play and, within this, another disagreement as to what role the U. S. military should play. There has been too little recognition of the fact that Americans are far more efficient at civic action than the Vietnamese officialdom. They are more aggressive, more resourceful, more compassionate and less venal and, of the Americans, the military is best suited, by organization, to do this job. All they need are Vietnamese with them, to help distinguish friend from foe.

Only the most modest beginning has been made in this area so far. In the absence of fully adequate authoritative direction from above, U. S. and RVN civil and military forces in I Corps have gotten together in a "Joint Coordinating Council" to sort out responsibilities and to move aggressively toward bringing the promised better life to the people. This sui generis effort is bearing fruit. Pacification in I Corps is a unified effort and should become a national model.

Second is the matter of military priority. There has been too much generalized talk that "the first priority is destruction of the VC/PAVN main force" on the theory that, once this is done, rural tranquility will automatically emerge. This is idle. It has hurt us gravely already. RVN military and paramilitary resources, which are very limited, are constantly being expended maneuvering about the country, reacting to the initiatives of VC main force units, while the people-- literally millions of them--are left essentially naked, to be violated and subverted by the guerrillas.

This is not to say that we should not take the offensive to hurt or destroy main force elements, when circumstances are abundantly in our favor, or that we will not find it necessary to engage them to prevent damage to population centers or invasion of rice-rich areas.

However, it is intended here to say, without qualification, that if the enemy cannot get to the people, he cannot win, and it is therefore the people whom we must protect as a matter of first business. We are not now doing it. Vietnamese manpower programs, Vietnamese and U. S. military tactics, are not now aimed primarily at that part of the enemy who is propagandizing, subverting, terrorizing and--in a real sense--capturing the people, but are pointed at a target farther remote.

Thus, it is concluded that until we reorient our strategy more directly upon the people and their local security, the battle is not going to go well for us. It will be said that the manpower requirements to bring reasonable protection to 14, 000 villages promise to be very great. That is correct. However, it is put in better perspective by two comments. First, the requirements, while certainly large, will be met more and more from manpower resources uncovered by progress in the tranquilization program itself. Second, large as the personnel demands are, they are dwarfed by the prospects of trying to fight a battle of manpower attrition against seven hundred million Asians--which is where we seem to be headed now.

VI. A U.S. Strategy

1. The preceding sections, in brief terms, seek to underscore the essentials of the war, as it really is. From the points made therein, the following three-cornered strategy emerges:

   I. Shift the thrust of the GVN and U. S. ground effort to the task of delivering the people from guerrilla oppression, and to protecting them adequately and continually thereafter; meanwhile seeking out and attacking main force elements when the odds can be made overwhelmingly in our favor.

   II. Address our attritional efforts primarily to the source of DRV material introduction, fabrication and distribution, close the ports, destroy the rail lines, destroy power, fuel and heavy industry, while deemphasizing the armed reconnaissance program as too diffuse and marginally productive.

III. Put the full weight of our top level effort into bringing all applicable resources—U. S. and GVN—into the pacification process. Create a single combined organization that acknowledges openly and exploits the usefulness of U. S, military participation in pacification, while using whatever leverage is available, to move the GVN to undertake an immediate agrarian reform program.

2. The responsive plan of campaign should encompass the following actions, listed under the three strategic points enumerated above:

I. Shift the effort to delivering and protecting the people.

A, Execute the phase II and IIa deployments; seek more third country participation; press the GVN for manpower improvements which will reduce diffusion of resources, and see more men productively employed under arms.

B. Secure the U. S. base areas, putting maximum possible reliance on mechanical security, in order to free manpower for offensive employment.

C. In conjunction with the RVNAF, initiate expanding clearing operations from these base areas as well as from the Saigon area, aimed at creating steadily growing geographic regions which are generally free of Viet Cong influence. Extend these clearing operations to commence denial of the foodstuffs there to the Mekong Delta to the Viet Cong.

D. Devote whatever resources are necessary, in military and paramilitary force, to the task of protecting the people in the areas cleared, along with their crops and institutions, from subversion and guerrilla action. Under no circumstances remove military and paramilitary protection until police protection is adequate.

E. Combine comint, ellnt, photo, clandestine, covert and other intelligence programs for the specific purpose of locating accurately the concentrations of enemy main force units, headquarters, supply and training areas. Attack them continuously by air, and at a very much higher level than at present. Attack main force elements on the ground when the convergence of intelligence establish that the benefits promise to be overwhelmingly in our favor, and when to do so will not consume forces needed for protection of cleared areas.

Courageous Dissent

        F. Intensify psychological warfare campaigns, utilizing heavily the services of defectors and Chieu Hoi ralliers, and aimed directly at the morale of the VC.

        II. (Address attritional efforts primarily to the DRV sources of material introduction and production).

        A. Without any further warning destroy

        (1) Major DRV POL storage areas.

        (2) The Haiphong, Hon Gay and Vinh port areas. Mine the ports.

        (3) The Haiphong River dredges.

        (4) The rail lines to South China.

        B. Follow the foregoing with a comprehensive psychological warfare campaign aimed at the North Vietnamese people, designed to diminish their support of the war, and to persuade the leadership that the cost will continue to rise.

        C. Proceed, unless contraindicated, with destruction of DRV power sources, heavy industry, coal, chemical and tin production.

        D. Seek, by convergence of all intelligence means, including intensive ground reconnaissance in Laos, to discover key way-points in the VC supply distribution system. Attack them by air continually, and in great strength. Attack them with ground sabotage forces.

        III. Converge all possible resources in the pacification process.

        A. Organize, uniformly, at the Saigon level, and in each Corps tactical zone, joint councils which coalesce the GVN and U.S. military and civilian efforts in a single program which aims to bring health, literacy, agricultural plenty and political awareness to the people.

        B. In execution use U. S. and GVN forces together.

        C. Increase, many fold, the level of medical assistance, accelerating the current U.S. civilian medical program and obliging all U. S. military units to contribute.

        D. Increase the level of popular forces training and compensation. Utilize U. S. forces, as necessary to support the training program.

        E. Direct, in specific terms, the conduct of comprehensive military civic action programs by all U.S. armed forces which have contact with the people.

F. Press the GVN to move immediately into a major land reform program to forgive back taxes, distribute excess lands and give prompt and tangible assurance that the program will reach every peasant.

IV. Conclusion.

This brief appraisal makes only two basic points which, in the context of achieving victory in Vietnam, are ineludible.—

First, no military strategy will promise success unless it gives full discount to the non-military factors of politics, economics and sociology.

And second, manpower being the enemy's area of greatest strength, we have no license and less reason to join battle with him on that ground. The changes in thrust proposed herein are designed around the conviction that scrupulous attention to these two facts is a design for victory, and evasion of their implications is the route to defeat.

Courageous Dissent

Appendix C

Letter of Non-Concurrence
October 1966

Maj. Gen. Wood Kyle's letter of non-concurrence regarding Barrier Concept

HEADQUARTERS
3d Marine Division (Rein) FMF
FPO San Francisco 96602

3/WRM/pnc
3300
003B30366
SECRET-NOFORN

From: Commanding General, 3d Marine Division
To: Commanding General, III Marine Amphibious Force

Subj: COMUSMACV Concept for Conduct of Defensive Operations in the vicinity of the DMZ(U)

Ref: (A) AC/S, MAC J3 Secret DF of date unknown, Subj: Outline Concept of Defensive Operations in the Vicinity of the DMZ (U)
(B) AC/S, MAC J4 SECRET DF MACDC-P/J4 of 13 Oct 66, Subject: Logistics Aspects of Task Force 728 Project - COMUSMACV Concept ©
(C) MACJ321 SECRET NOFORN Memorandum of date unknown, Subj: Barrier Study Conference

1. References (a) and (b) have been reviewed in light of the specific tasks assigned to III MAF in reference ©. Assuming the concept as finally received from COMUSMACV is essentially an expansion of the same concept advanced in reference (a), the following pertinent comments are provided:

Appendices

a. Non-concur in the Tab F concept of the 1st ARVN Division and elements of III MAF (presumably the 3d Marine Division) providing depth to the barrier defense system by being prepared to block, counterattack or eliminate enemy threats to the defensive area. Such an approach is considered to engage the only possible major advantage of existence of the barrier system; namely, the release of the combined forces of the 1st ARVN Division and 3d Marine Division for a much needed expansion of tactical operations and revolutionary development activities in southern QUANG TRI Province and throughout THUA TIEN Province. It would appear that the logistical expense of installing the barrier system and attendant development of supporting airfield and seaport facilities is such as to justify an accompanying provision of sufficient barrier defense forces to perform all operational tasks incident to employment of that system. In this connection, it is considered that a Barrier Defense Force of two divisions (in lieu of one division plus an armored cavalry regiment) is required to adequately provide for screening forces, outposts and patrols north of the barrier, forces to man the barrier system proper, forces for immediate reaction to attempted penetrations, and forces in depth to block, counterattack, and exploit the counterattack.

b. Non-concur in the Tab G inference that a Marine regiment may be required in a portion of the western sector of the barrier defense system. As stated in the previous paragraph, existence of the barrier defense system should free Marine forces for operations elsewhere - not freeze such forces in a barrier-watching defensive role.

c. It is considered that the provision of a northern QUANG TRI defensive force consisting of two divisions, as recommended above to accompany the barrier system and exclusive of 1st ARVN Division and 3d Marine Division assets, would in itself preclude the necessity for existence of the barrier system. In short, it is considered that two divisions are required in that area regardless of the existence of the barrier system. In the western sector, it is possible to conceive of more troops being required by the existence of the barrier system than would be required without it. Screening, patrolling, and reconnaissance force requirements would be about equal in either case; reaction force requirements might be less with the barrier system; but any reduction in reaction forces could be counterbalanced by force requirements to man the barrier itself, which forces would be "locked" in place and hence of little use elsewhere. When the additional forces to maintain the defile barriers and connecting roads are considered, it is difficult to avoid the conclusion that a mobile and flexible defense by two divisions would be more efficient and cost effective than the participation of like forces in conjunction with a barrier system. The development of airfield and port facilities at DONG HA and HUE to support a two-division mobile defense force would certainly be far less than the extensive effort required to support the proposed barrier construction plus the 1 and 1/3 division defense force envisaged.

d. If the barrier system concept is pursued, a completely separate Barrier Defense Command should be established in the vicinity of DONG HA at the very outset of the development and construction program involved. Whether such a Command is to be under OPCON III MAF, or a separate Command directly under COMUSMACV, is obviously a matter for joint III MAF COMUSMACV resolution. In any event, such a Command should progressively exercise complete control and coordination of all operational and logistical forces involved in the planning, construction, defense, and support of segments of the barrier system as they are constructed from east-to-west. As U.S. Army and ROK elements are introduced into the area, specific lines of demarcation should be established on the ground to clearly delineate between Barrier Defense Command and Marine Division areas of responsibility. As the Barrier Defense Command area of responsibility westward, and Marine Division tactical operations should shift westward and Southward. When the entire barrier defense system is completed and fully manned and supported by the Barrier Defense Command, a specific NE-to-SW line of demarcation should be established on the ground to clearly delineate between the Barrier Defense Command area of responsibility and the tactical area of operations of the 3d Marine Division in the remainder of QUANG TRI Province. Such a Barrier Defense Command is foreseen to include a major logistics force, and to operate as a completely separate entity from the 3rd Marine Division and, possibly, any other elements of III MAF.

Appendices

e. If the barrier system concept is pursued, each of the strong points contemplated in the western sector of the proposed barrier line is considered to require an infantry company for round-the-clock operations. It is not difficult to foresee a requirement at any given time for one platoon to be patrolling northward and laterally, one platoon to be manning the strong point, and one platoon resting, cleaning weapons, and preparing to assume one of the aforementioned functions. Anything less than one company per strong point would reduce patrolling and reconnaissance capabilities and invite a rapid enemy penetration of the line with less than adequate warning and untimely deployment of reaction forces from the rear. In short, early warning and resistance capabilities must exist at the strong point itself, and the provision of such capabilities requires a company at each strong point. Since about 16 of the 27 companies of a division would be involved in the manning of the strong points, some 11 companies would remain for screening operations to the north and as reaction forces in the rear. This is considered to lend support to the contention that two divisions would really be required in support of a defense line all the way from the LAOS border to the east coast, with 15 percent of the total force being required in the western sector (west of the north-south grid line 03).

f. If the barrier system concept is pursued, every defile barrier, strong point, and connecting road in the western sector will have to be covered by artillery and/or mortar fire, since air support cannot be relied upon in the poor weather and visibility conditions which prevail in that area. This will necessitate an east-to-west spreading of artillery assets throughout the western sector, and produce attendant problems of security for the artillery units. Again there is a dissipation of forces available for screening and reaction purposes, and support of the probable need of a greater density of forces in the western sector.

g. Whether the barrier system concept is pursued or is discarded in favor of a two-division mobile defense as recommended herein, an extensive engineer effort is considered to be required along the following lines.

(1) Upgrading Route 9 to a first rate, two lane MSR all the way from DONG HA to KHE SANH.

(2) Doubling the capacity of Route 1 from PHU BAI through DONG HA and north to the vicinity of GIO LINH.

(3) Construction of two alternate two-lane routes eastward from Route 1 to the embark/debark point at the mouth of the COA VIE! water-way, one emanating from DONG HA, the other from QUANG TRI.

(4) Construction of a first rate route from the vicinity of the city of QUANG TRI through the BA LONG Valley to join Route 9 at CA LU.

(5) Upgrading of the unloading and clearing facilities at the embark/debark points at DONG HA and at the mouth of the CUA VIET waterway, to the level of a major port.

h. The engineer effort described in the preceding paragraph, coupled with a two-division mobile defense concept for northern QUANG TRI Province, offers greater potential benefits for far less engineer effort than the proposed barrier defense system.

Appendix D

Exit Interview, Q&A Session
January 1967

Excerpt from Brig. Gen. Lowell English's exit interview as Assistant Division Commander, 3rd Marine Division, Vietnam. General English had recently returned from Vietnam. He had served as ADC for the 3rd Marine Division until 6 January 1967. He was interviewed by Marine Officers in the G1, G2, G3 and G4 sections. The interview was classified as "Secret."

Now to Khe Sanh.
Any outpost that is as far away from things as KS is vulnerable... But the fact that it is far away from everything makes me wonder just exactly how important it is to the enemy? We've had a lot of anxiety about another Dien Bien Phu, and that this might very well be an opportunity for them to mount an offensive, gain a significant victory that has a psychological advantage to them.

The truth of the matter is when you get to Khe Sanh, you're not anyplace really. You can't hurt anybody, you've got to move from Khe Sanh someplace else to hurt anybody really. It's kind of like having the VC units back in the mountains. They are not hurting you, as long as they stay in the mountains.

KS is an important symbol, but it isn't any more important than A Shau was as far as the overall effort is concerned. It has to be looked at from the standpoint of: do we want to extend the effort that is necessary to protect KS? It's a symbol. It's a question: do we want to take the risk that it is going to be attacked or perhaps overrun and if you want to keep it, then you better not put less than a battalion over there with the artillery - that is a minimum. If you cut it below that then you are just asking for trouble.

And we are supposed to open up the road from Ca Lu to KS. The only thing I can say about that is that I don't know who the hell is going to use it? Or for what purpose? You are certainly not going to try and supply a battalion over that road I hope, because it would take a regiment to be damn sure that your trucks got through. We built an airfield out there, we've got GCA in there. You can resupply the thing by air. So the real reason for opening Route 9 up was to support a division. That wasn't ever our idea; it was the Army's idea. We're still stuck with it.

But, as far as KS is concerned, I think you could lose it and you wouldn't have lost a damned thing.

Any other questions?

Appendices

Appendix E

Presidential Unit Citation, Dewey Canyon
1969

By virtue of the authority vested in me as President of the United States and as Commander in Chief of the Armed Forces of the United States, I have today awarded

THE PRESIDENTIAL UNIT CITATION (ARMY)

FOR EXTRAORDINARY HEROISM TO THE 9TH MARINE REGIMENT 3RD MARINE DIVISION UNITED STATES MARINE CORPS AND ATTACHED UNITS

The assigned and attached units of the 9th Marine Regiment, 3rd Marine Division distinguished themselves by extraordinary heroism, professionalism, and achievement in military action against the North Vietnamese Army in the Da Krong and Northern A Shau Valleys, Quang Tri Providence, Republic of Vietnam, during the period 22 January to 18 March 1969. Launched under the code name "Dewey Canyon" the concept of the eight-week offensive was a thrust deep into the enemy's rear area and to destroy a heretofore impregnable major base. A week of inclement weather delayed the surprise attack and halted combat support, resupply, and medical evacuation. When the weather cleared to the extent that the helicopters operations were possible, the Marines found that the enemy had skillfully exploited the delay to strengthen his defenses, position medium range artillery, and otherwise complete preparation of the battlefield. Undaunted, the Marines and their South Vietnamese counterparts drove southward, enduring intense artillery, mortar, and automatic weapons fire, to rout a determined enemy from his fortifications. The Marines repulsed numerous counterattacks in the process of decimating the equivalent of two North Vietnamese Army Regiments. The 9th Marine Regiment and its attached units destroyed the enemy's regional command control apparatus, eliminated a series of headquarters establishments, and inflicted over 1600 casualties on the North Vietnamese Army. The enemy's engineer and transport capabilities were severely diminished. Additionally, the Marines captured over 1000 tons of weapons, equipment and supplies; including individual weapons, Infantry crew-served weapons, antiaircraft guns, Field Artillery pieces, vehicles, small-caliber ammunition, and rice. As a result of their gallant actions, the North Vietnamese Army Spring Offensive in the I Corps Tactical Zone was preempted. This magnificent feat of arms, achieved against severe odds and seemingly insurmountable obstacles was made possible by the extraordinary courage, skill, cohesion, and fighting spirit of the 9th Marine Regiment, 3rd Marine Division and its attached units. The superb performance of the officers and men of this force represents the essence of professionalism, is in keeping with the highest traditions of the military service, and reflects great credit on them and the Armed Forces of the United States.

Richard Nixon

Author's Note

During the writing of this book, we had many discussions regarding our experiences in Vietnam, in the Marine Corps, and new things that we learned. We researched and debated concepts, timelines, places, and names—also, the important topic of leadership. One recurring question: What if the War Managers in Washington and Saigon had listened to our dissenters and acted on their recommendations? Some questions and discussions were not part of the story we planned to tell. One question is the decision-making process. What if:

In his 1965 Press Conference, the President had honestly described the nation's risks in Vietnam. He would have articulated the national security threats if we failed to act, and also the potential for escalation to a war that cost millions of lives. The patience of the war-weary American public might have increased, giving time to negotiate a peaceful settlement with North Vietnam.

In 1966, the President had challenged the strategy of a war of attrition and advocated instead a version of the enclave strategy. The city of Hue would have likely been included in the Phu Bai enclave, surrounded by villages with combined action (Vietnamese & American) units. U.S. and South Vietnamese casualties would have been significantly reduced. Body counts would have not been needed to assess the progress of the war. The successful NVA Army attack and bloody battle of Hue during the 1968 Tet Offensive might have been avoided.

In 1966, the Secretary of Defense had abandoned the idea of an anti-infiltration barrier across the DMZ, and south to Khe Sanh. Instead, the US military would have chosen an "active defense" strategy and identified a line of defense from Dong Ha to the Rock Pile or Ca Lu, out of range of NVA artillery. The October 1966 barrier conference would have been an "NVA Base area" conference. The defense of Khe Sanh Combat Base might have been avoided.

In 1967, the Commanding General MACV might have avoided the "border fights" including Dak To, Loc Ninh, Song be, Con Thien, and the first battle of Khe Sanh. Instead of search and destroy in the mountains, the warfighting would have centered on the coastal enclaves and the NVA Base areas along the Laos border. Tactics would have been similar to Operation Pegasus and Dewey Canyon, employing helicopters and high mobility used by Army divisions including the First Air Cavalry. Strategic bombing of North Vietnam would be replaced by saturation bombing of the NVA Base areas along the unpopulated Laos border, avoiding population centers.

In 1968, with the shift in war-fighting strategy, the TET offensive could have been significantly reduced by interdicting NVA lines of communication that connected the Ho Chi Minh Trail in Laos to the coastal Vietnam cities. There would have been no defense of Khe Sanh Combat Base in 1968, saving a thousand lives.

By following the recommendations of our dissenters, it is possible that millions of lives could have been saved; both Southeast Asian and American. The outcome of the Vietnam War might have changed. Regrettably, we will never know.

Glossary

Arc Light—The codename for B-52 bombing missions in South Vietnam.

AK-47 — Russian-made Kalashnikov automatic rifle, gas operated, uses 7.62mm ammunition.

B-52 — Boeing Stratofortress, U.S. Air wing, heavy jet bomber.

Battery — Military unit designated by letters within the parent battalion, eg. Echo Battery, 2nd Battalion, 12th Marines. During the Vietnam War, normally commanded by a Captain and consisted of six gun sections, as well as fire direction, communications, and transport sections. A direct-support relationship existed between the 12th Marines and the 9th Marines.

C-123—US Air Force transport aircraft for personnel and aircraft delivery of supplies.

C- 130— Lockheed Hercules, aircraft. a four-engine turboprop transport.

Casualty — Personnel who are no longer available to a unit: killed, wounded, captured, missing.
CH-46 Marine Helicopter Sea Stallion, for transport of Personnel, cargo, and light/medium artillery.

CH- 53 — Sikorsky Sea Stallion, a single-rotor, heavy assault transport helicopter.

Company — Military unit designated by letters within the parent battalion, eg. Hotel Company, 2nd Battalion, 9th Marines. Within Marine infantry during the Vietnam War, normally commanded by a Captain and consisting of three rifle platoons and one weapons platoon.

Combined action program—A Marine pacification program established at Phu Bai in August 1965 which integrated a Marine infantry squad with a South Vietnamese Popular Forces platoon.

G—Refers to staff positions on a general staff, e. g., G-1 would refer to the staff member responsible for personnel; G-2 intelligence; G-3 operations; G-4 logistics. For staff

positions below the general level an S- is used.
Gun, 175mm, M107—U.S. built, self-propelled gun maximum range of 32,800 meters.
Gun, 155mm, M53—U.S. built, medium, self-propelled gun. with a 23,300-meter range.
Howitzer, 8-inch (M55)— U.S. built, self-propelled heavy-artillery piece range of 16,800 meters.
Howitzer, 105mm, M101A1—U.S. built, towed, artillery piece with a maximum range of 11,500 meters.
Howitzer, 155mm—both the M-114A towed and M-109 self-propelled artillery piece with a maximum range of 15,000 meters.
Howtar—A 4.2-inch (107mm) mortar tube mounted on the frame of a 75mm pack howitzer.
"Huey" — Popular name for the UH-1 series of helicopters.
I Corps—Operational subdivision that includes the five northern provinces of South Vietnam.
JASON—an independent group of Scientists organized by the Pentagon to advise on scientific matters.
KC-135—Robert McNamara's aircraft; a model that served primarily as a refueling tanker but existed in several variants including as a command station.
Marines—Designates a Marine regiment, e.g. 3d Marines.
Mortar, 4.2-inch, M30—U.S. built, rifled, muzzle-loaded, drop-fired weapon range of 4,020 meters.
Mortar, 81mm, M29—U.S. built, smooth-bore, muzzle-loaded, single-shot, high angle of fire weapon with a range of approximately 5,000 meters.
Mortar, 82mm—Soviet-built, smooth-bore, muzzle-loaded, single-shot, high-angle of fire weapon and a range of about 5,000 meters.
Mortar, 120mm—Soviet or Chinese Communist built, smooth bore, drop or trigger fired with a range of 5,700 meters.
Practice Nine—The codename for the planning of the anti-infiltration barrier across the DMZ.
Rolling Thunder—Codename for U.S. air operations over North Vietnam.

List of Abbreviations

ARVN—Army of the Republic of Vietnam (South Vietnam).
ASRT—Air support radar team.
BGen—Brigadier general.
BLT—Battalion landing team.
Bn—Battalion.
ADC—Assistant division commander.
Capt—Captain.
CINCPAC—Commander in Chief Pacific, U.S. Navy Commander, a four-star admiral
CMC—Commandant of the Marine Corps.
CNO—Chief of Naval Operations.
CO—Commanding officer. **Col** — Colonel.
CAP—Combined action program
ComdC—Command chronology.
ComUSMACV—Commander, U.S. Military Assistance Command, Vietnam.
CORDS—Office of Civil Operations and Rural Support, organized in May 1967
COSVN—Central Office of South Vietnam, the Communist military and political headquarters
CTZ—Corps Tactical Zone.
DMZ— Demilitarized Zone separating North and South Vietnam.
DRV—Democratic Republic of Vietnam (North Vietnam).
Div— Division.
DOD—Department of Defense.
DOW—Died of Wounds
FDC—Fire Direction Center. An element within artillery regiments, battalions, and batteries that was tasked with developing gun data, target information, and command and control of direct artillery fire support.
FLC—Force Logistic Command.
FSB— Fire Support Base.
FSCC—Fire support coordination center, a single location in

which were centralized communication facilities and personnel incident to the coordination of all forms of fire support.
Gen—General.
GVN—Government of Vietnam (South Vietnam).
HASC—House Armed Services Committee.
H&S Co—Headquarters and service company.
HistBr, G-3Div, HQMC—Historical Branch, G-3 Division, Headquarters, U.S. Marine Corps.
H&I—Harassing and interdicting artillery fire.
HQMC—Headquarters Marine Corps.
HQ—Headquarters.
ILT—First Lieutenant
ICM—Improved conventional munitions that consist of a mechanical time fuze and a body assembly containing a number of submunitions.
III MAF—III Marine Amphibious Force.
JCS—Joint Chiefs of Staff.
KSCB—Khe Sanh Combat Base.
KIA—Killed-in-action.
LCVP—Landing Craft Vehicle and Personnel.
Lt—Lieutenant.
LtCol—Lieutenant colonel.
LtGen—Lieutenant general.
LZ— Landing Zone for a helicopter.
MajGen—Major general.
MarDiv—Marine division.
MACV—Military Assistance Command, Vietnam..
MAF—Marine amphibious force.
MAG—Marine aircraft group.
Maj—Major.
NSC—National Security Council.
NKP—Nakhon Phanom Thailand.
NVA—North Vietnamese Army.
PF—Popular Force, Vietnamese militia.
POL—Petroleum, oil, and lubricants.
PAVN—People's Army of Vietnam (North Vietnam).
PROVN—Pacification and Long Term Development of South Vietnam, a program designed by the U.S. Army, never

approved nor implemented.
RF—Regional Force, Vietnamese militia who were employed in a specific area.
Regt—Regiment.
ROK—Republic of Korea (South Korea).
RPG—Rocket-Propelled Grenade.
RVNAF—Republic of Vietnam Air Force.
SID—Seismic Intrusion Device.
SACSA—Special Assistant for Counterinsurgency and Special Activities, reporting to President Kennedy.
SAVA—Special Assistant Vietnam, Senior CIA official.
SVN—South Viet Nam.
TCK/TKN—North Vietnamese acronym, translated to General Offensive, General Uprising.
USS—United States Ship.
WIA—Wounded in Action.
WSAG—Washington Special Action Group, organized to manage Operation Lam Son 719.
XO—Executive Officer.

Bibliography

2nd Battalion, 12th Marine Regiment Feb 1969, *Command chronology*, National Archives Catalog. http: www.catalog.archives.gov

(No author) "An Alliance Personified," The New York Times, Oct 3, 1959

(No author) "Fightin' 9th Nails 352 NVA." Sea Tiger, Vol. 5, No. 9. III Marine Amphibious Brigade. February 28, 1969.

(No author) "Letter From the Ambassador to Laos (Sullivan) to the Assistant Secretary of State for Far Eastern Affairs (Bundy)." Vientiane, October 17, 1966. Source: Department of State.

(No author) "NVA Lose 1,355 Dead, Munitions Top 500 Tons." Sea Tiger, Vol. 5, No. 13. III Marine Amphibious Brigade. March 28, 1969.

(No author) *The Pentagon Papers* Gravel Edition Volume 4 "The Air War in North Vietnam, 1965-1968," Boston: Beacon Press, 1971

Andrew, Rod Jr. *The First Battle of Khe Sanh, 1967*. U.S.M.C History Division, Marine Corps University, Quantico, Virginia, 2017.

Archer, Michael. "Interview." Conducted by Robert A. Packard. 19 August 2020.

Archer, Michael. *The Gunpowder Prince: How Marine Corps Captain Mirza Munir Baig Saved Khe Sanh*. Independently Published, 2018.

Archer, Michael. *The Long Goodbye: Khe Sanh Revisited*. Ashland, OR: Hellgate Press, 2016.

Braestrup, Peter. *Big Story: How the American Press and Television Reported and Interpreted the Crisis of TET 1968 in Vietnam and Washington*. New Haven, Yale University Press, 1977.

Brush, Peter. "The Battle of Khe Sanh, 1968" in The Tet Offensive, ed Marc Jason Gilbert and William Head.

Westport, CT: Greenwood Publishing Group. 1996.
Buzzanco, Robert. *Three Generals & the Viet Nam War: Essays Vietnam Generation*. Burning Cities Press, 1992
Buzzanco, Robert. *Masters of War: Military Dissent and Politics in the Vietnam Era*. Cambridge University Press, 1996
Callahan, Shawn P. Close *Air Support and the Battle for Khe Sanh*. Quantico, VA History Division, Marine Corps University, 2009.
Camp, Richard. *Three Marine War Hero*. Hagerstown: CASEMATE publishers, 2019.
Camp, Richard. "Taking Command: A Lesson in Leadership." Marine Corps Gazette, June 1999
Camp, Richard D. and Blasiol, Leonard A. *Ringed by Fire: U.S. Marines and the Siege of Khe Sanh 21 January to 9 July 1968*. Quantico, VA. History Division, Marine Corps University, 2019.
Coolidge, Robert. *Veterans History Project*. Washington DC: Library of Congress, 2011.
Correll, John T., "All Eyes on Khe Sanh", In Air Force Magazine, March (2016)
Correll, John. "Igloo White" Air Force Magazine, 2004
Craig, Thomas B. Maj U.S. Army, "Leveraging the Power of Loyal Dissent in the U.S. Army," Military Review, November-December 2014.
Davis, Gordon M. "Dewey Canyon: All Weather Classic," Marine Corps Gazette 53, 1969
Davis, Raymond G. *The Story of Ray Davis: General of Marines*, Fuquay Varuna NC, Research Triangle Publishing, 1995.
Drea, Edward. *McNamara, Clifford, and the Burdens of Vietnam 1965-1969*. Washington, D.C. Secretaries of Defense Historical Series, 2011
Drennan, Jimmy, Lieutenant Commander USN, "Bad Ideas Have No Rank: The Moral Imperative of Dissent in the Navy," USNI Proceedings, July 2019.
Eggleston, Michael. *Dak To and the Border Battles of Vietnam, 1967-1968*, Jefferson, NC: McFarland & Company, 2017.
English, Lowell. "Interview FMPPAC Q&A session 8 January 1967." Quantico, VA: USMCU, 1982
Finkbeiner, Ann K. *The Jasons: The Secret History of Science's*

Postwar Elite. New York: Penguin, 2006.
Fisher, Roger. "Obituary. " Harvard Law Today. 2012
Fisher, Roger and William Ury with Bruce Patton, Editor. *Getting to YES: Negotiating an agreement without giving in. USA:* Penguin. 2011
Ford, Ronnie. "Hanoi's Intent: Khe Sanh and the Tet Offensive "American Intelligence Journal, National Military Intelligence Foundation Autumn/Winter (1995)
Fournier, Ismaël "Hybrid Warfare in Vietnam: The U.S. And South Vietnamese Success Against the Viet Cong." Marine Corps History Vol 7, No 1.
Genkel, Alfred N., 1stLt. "Clerks Stop NVA Sapper Attack." Sea Tiger, Vol. 5, No. 11. III Marine Amphibious Brigade. March 14, 1969.
Givens, Seth. *On Our Terms: U.S. Marines in Operation Dewey Canyon, 22 January to 18 March 1969.* Quantico: Marine Corps History Division, 2021.
Gibbons,William, *The U.S. Government and the Vietnam War: Executive and Legislative Roles:* New Jersey, Princeton University Press, 1995.
Greene, Wallace, "Memorandum for Record, first meeting of JCS with HASC, July 15, 1965, "Quantico: USMCU, 1965.
Greene, Wallace, "Notes of Meeting July 22, 1965, SEA Committee." http://www.history.state.gov
Herring, George "Cold War and Vietnam." *OAH Magazine of History,* Vol. 18, No. 5, Vietnam (Oct., 2004), pp. 18-21.
Herring, George, America's Longest War: The United States and Vietnam, 1950-1975 5th Ed. McGraw Hill Education, 2013.
Holland, William J. Jr., Rear Admiral USN (Ret.). "Dissent Is Not Disloyalty". USNI Proceedings, July 2003.
Huntington, Samuel P. *The Soldier and the State*, Harvard University Press, 1957 Internal Defense and Development Committee, Vietnam Information Booklet. Tactics Group, Brigade and Battalion Operations Department, U. S. Army Infantry School. Issued by the U. S. Army Artillery and Missile School, Fort Sill, Oklahoma, November 1967,
Karnow, Stanley *Vietnam: A history the First Complete account of*

Vietnam at War New York, The Viking Press, WGBH Educational Foundation, 1983.
Kinnard, Douglas. *Adventures in Two Worlds*. USA: XLibris, 2012
Krulak, Victor, *First to Fight*, Annapolis: Naval Institute Press, 1984
Metzger, Louis, "McNamara's Wall "Marine Corps Gazette; Sep 1999.
Milburn, Andrew R. "Breaking Ranks: Dissent and the Military Professional." US Army News and Information, October 26, 2010.
Morrison, William. Barrier Plan III MAF Conference, 3RD MARDIV *Command Chronology* OCT66 Maryland: National Records Archives, 1966
Murray, Nicholas "More Dissent Needed: Critical thinking and Professional Military education." Blogs Charlie Mike. July 29, 2014.
Nevgloski, Edward. *The United States Marines' Strategy and Approach to the Conventional War in South Vietnam's Northern Provinces, March 1965—December 1967*. PhD dissertation, King's College, 2019
Neville, R.B. III MAF *Command Chronology* OCT66. Maryland: National Record Archives, 1966
O'Connell, Aaron. "Review of Gregory Daddis, *Withdrawal: Re-Assessing America's Final Years in Vietnam*" Quantico, Marine Corps University Press, 2021
Palmer, Bruce Jr *The Twenty-five year War: America's Military Role in Vietnam*, Lexington, KY: University of Kentucky Press, 1984,
Phillips, Ross Eldridge. *Operation Dewey Canyon: Search and Destroy in the Age of Abrams*, Master's Thesis, Texas A&M University, 2019.
Pisor, Robert L. *The End of the Line: The Siege of Khe Sanh*. New York, W. W. Norton & Company, 1982.
Prados, John. *Vietnam: The History of an Unwinnable War, 1945-1975*. University Press of Kansas 2009.
Prados, John and Ray Stubbe. *Valley of Decision: The Siege of Khe Sanh*. Boston: Houghton Mifflin, 1991.
Rayburn, James S. "Direct Support During Operation Dewey

Canyon." The NAVSECGRU Bulletin, Vol. XXIV, No. 11, Nov/Dec 1980

Sheehan, Neil, *The Pentagon Papers*, New York: Quadrangle Books, 1971

Sheehan, Neal. *A Bright Shining Lie*. New York: Random House, 1988.

Shore, Moyers S. *The Battle for Khe Sanh*. USMC History and Museums Division, U.S. Marine Corps, Washington, D.C. 1969

Shulimson, Jack. *U. S. Marines in Vietnam: An Expanding War, 1966*. Washington, D.C. History and Museums Division, HQMC, 1982.

Shuster Alvin, William Colby. "U.S. Chief of Pacification for Vietnam, Gives Up Duties and Returns Home," New York Times, July 1, 1971

Snider, Don M. "Dissent and Strategic Leadership of the Military Professions." US Army War College USAWC, February 2008.

Summers, Harry G. *On Strategy: The Vietnam War in Context*. Carlisle Barracks, PA. Strategic Studies Institute, 1981.

Telfer, Gary and Lane Rogers, Keith Fleming. *Fighting the North Vietnamese 1967*. Washington DC: HQMC History and Museums, 1984

Vaughn, David, and James Donohoe. *From Stalingrad to Khe Sanh: Factors in the Successful Use of Tactical Airlift to Support Isolated Land Battle Areas*. Air Force Institute of Technology, undated but post-1998.

Vietnam Task Force, Office of the Secretary of Defense. *United States-Vietnam Relations, 1945–1967* (The Pentagon Papers). 1969

Weiner, Tim. "Robert S. McNamara, Architect of a Futile War, Dies at 93," New York Times, July 6, 2009

Westmoreland, William C. *A Soldier Reports*. Garden City NY. Da Capo paperback, 1976

Wirtz, James "A Review Essay of H.R. McMaster's *Dereliction of Duty*" Political Science Quarterly 134 1999

Acknowledgements

I owe a deep debt of gratitude to those who helped me write this book. All are former Marines, all served together in the same military organization: the 9th Marine Expeditionary Brigade (MEB), built around the 9th Marine Regiment and the 2nd Battalion 12th Marine Regiment. In 1965, they were the first combat troops to land in Vietnam; in 1969, the first to depart.

I am very grateful to Dr. John Cochenour. John and his wife Donnice are dear friends for more than fifty years. We met at the Marine Officers' Basic School (TBS), served together in Vietnam, and later in Hawaii. After the Marines, John switched gears to academia. His second career was in Instructional Technology. As a professor, he supervised more than 100 doctoral candidates writing dissertations, and was recognized as a Professor Emeritus. He brought his experience and unique insight to writing and publishing this book.

I am indebted to Robert Packard, friend in college, and usher in our wedding. We were fellow midshipmen at the Duke University NROTC unit. Bob is a career Marine, served in the Marine Corps for more than twenty years, and retired as a Lieutenant Colonel. His second career was with a defense contractor, where he sharpened his writing skills. Bob's military experience and writing skill is evident in the Khe Sanh chapter of this book.

I strongly and sincerely thank G.M. Davis, my oldest friend from high school. He grew up in a Marine family, (like me) a son of a Marine General. Our paths crossed twice in Vietnam—the second encounter was in a medical aide station, after his helicopter crashed at Fire Base Cunningham. His second career was as an attorney, and he retired as a federal magistrate judge. His book *My War in the Jungle* is an Amazon best seller. He wrote the Dewey Canyon chapter of this book. As a published author, his participation and help were invaluable.

The staff of the Marine Corps University at Quantico has been very helpful and supportive: Angela Anderson Director Marine Corps University Press, John Lyles, Archivist, Andy Hayt Archives Technician, Alisa Whitley, Branch Head and Archivist, and Fred Allison, head of Oral History. All were very friendly, very helpful and very professional. Multiple visits to the Marine Corps University library were extremely helpful. My last visit to Quantico produced a big surprise: the personal papers of

General Wallace Greene. Those papers had been unavailable for years during the de-classification process. Two of them - both Memoranda to file written by General Greene - are included in the Appendices to this book. Very few people have read them.

I want to also extend many thanks to our "beta readers:" Mike Miller, Jack Sammons, Clyde Davis, Tony Edgar, Ed Norton, and Dick Camp. A special thanks to Dick Camp for his thoughts on General Ray Davis. Camp served as General Davis' first aide in Vietnam from March to July 1968. Camp is also a prolific author. He has published more than 150 military oriented articles for various magazines, including Leatherneck, Marine Corps Gazette, Vietnam Magazine, World War II and Naval Institute Press. Dick is also the author of 14 books, including Echo Among Warriors, Storming the Point, and The Killing Ground. The input from all the readers was really appreciated and for sure has improved the book.

Mary Fetherston provided excellent yeoman service with her editing and suggestions in the final stages of our writing. Using her extensive military and editing experience from assignments at the Naval War College, Officer Candidate School and the University of Rhode Island, Mary was able to smooth out many inconsistencies and confusing spots within the manuscript. She served as a senior officer in the US Naval Reserve, retiring as a Captain. Chris Kyle also provided a fresh perspective and excellent suggestions to improve readability during the final drafting of the book. Chris is a film and TV writer who has written for Disney, Universal, Sony and ESPN. Chris graduated from Duke University and UCLA, where he received the Jack Nicholson, Abraham Polonsky, and Samuel Goldwyn screenwriting awards. He's been teaching at UCLA since 2011.

The encouragement, critique, and assistance received from everyone enabled me to turn an idea into a reality. Any mistakes are the result of the authors alone, and the best parts of this book should be credited to the these professionals who lent me their knowledge and support.

Most important of all. I again thank my wife Debbie. Without your love and support, this book would not have been possible.

A.S. Kyle 2023

Courageous Dissent

Made in the USA
Columbia, SC
20 March 2024